CW00406370

FOR SALE

25p

Jacqueline Buksh was born in Bradford, Yorkshire, educated in Cumbria and got her degrees and teacher's certificate in London. (Middlesex and London Universities.)

She taught at three schools in North London as a Primary teacher, Language specialist and school co-ordinator. Ninety eight percent of pupils she taught were from other countries.

Always keen on foreign culture and languages she travelled widely including Europe, Scandinavia, North Africa, Turkey, Russia (as it was then), and large parts of the Far East.

Jacqueline studied Chinese at The People's University in Beijing (Peking) and went on to work for two years for the UNDP (United Nations Development Programme) in Wuhan, China, followed by six years in Shenzhen, Guangdong, PR China. A total of fourteen years living and working in China.

She has written and edited a series of bilingual books and tapes which are used in schools throughout China; appeared several times on Chinese TV promoting her interactive style of teaching. Finally, Jacqueline left China to concentrate on family and writing whilst living in Blackpool.

# Fourteen
# Years in China

# Jacqueline Buksh

# Fourteen Years in China

Vanguard Press

VANGUARD PAPERBACK

© Copyright 2003
**Jacqueline Buksh**

A CIP catalogue record for this title is
available from the British Library
ISBN 1 843860 68 6


*Vanguard Press is an imprint of
Pegasus Elliot MacKenzie Publishers Ltd.*
www.pegasuspublishers.com


First Published in 2003

**Vanguard Press
Sheraton House  Castle Park
Cambridge  England**


Printed & Bound in Great Britain

# Dedication

To Karim; husband, travel and life's companion, with
grateful appreciation and love for all encouragement
and help with this book.

# Acknowledgement

To the United Nations Development Programme, for selecting me to teach at 'Hubei College of Traditional Medicine' in Wuchang.

To my friends and colleagues at 'Shenzhen Nanshan Foreign Languages School', and of course all my students, those lovely Chinese children whom I have had the great pleasure of teaching over many years.

To the 'Hwawei Telecommunications', Science and Industry Park, Shenzhen, the Futian International Bank, and Shenzhen University English College, for its lively and intelligent workers and diligent students of English.

Finally, grateful thanks to all those who made the publication of this book possible, I hope it may inspire others to spread their wings and explore another culture.

# Reasons for writing this book

The purpose of this book is to encapsulate all my years of travelling, living and working in China.

Most travel books are either about sponsored travel involving raising money for charities, or backpackers who hitchhike or live in tents. All noble ideals and often hair-raising from the safety of an armchair.

My book aims to show that extended travel is possible from age eighteen to eighty, for people who love to live and learn in another culture. Interesting travel is not confined to backpackers and a tent. Neither is it confined to a lot of money.

Initially you need enough to get to the country of your choice, enough to survive for a month if you do not have a prearranged job to go to. Young people can apply to do voluntary work, for which they can get enough to live on, at the same time experiencing their own personal adventures.

Older people can offer their skills and expertise in many different ways. To want to travel enough is to have a burning need inside which overcomes any difficulties, for example, finance, visas, injections and leaving family. To travel along is to find you are never alone! To travel with a group has its rewards and frustrations, each traveller must find their own personal way. I have tried all ways. Each is different, each is unique. For those willing to give of themselves time, knowledge and experience of life, and the ability to live at all levels from a student pad to a modest hostel, to their own rented accommodation and the odd bout of luxury. Life is what we make it, travel makes it wonderful! Learning from and helping others along the way is a privilege.

# Author's personal note

I hope I have conveyed to the reader some of the soul of China. It is an immense country with millions of people, most of them going about their daily lives in a fast growing economy and changing society. Not an easy life for many thousands but vibrant, young and rising, emerging like a butterfly from its chrysalis, it holds much promise for the future. Let us hope its power will lead in the best way for all.

# Contents

Introduction: Observations, Historical/Sociological

| | |
|---|---|
| Chapter 1 | First Visit to China 1987 |
| Chapter 2 | Teachers & Students |
| Chapter 3 | Teachers & Further Travels |
| Chapter 4 | Return to Beijing |
| Chapter 5 | Unknown Territory, Tibet |
| Chapter 6 | Beijing and Beidahe |
| Chapter 7 | VSO-UNDP and Wuhan (Traditional Chinese Medicine) |
| Chapter 8 | Cycles, Traffic, Exercise and an accident |
| Chapter 9 | Shenzhen (1995-2001) |
| Chapter 10 | Economy and Crime |
| Chapter 11 | Building and Neighbours |
| Chapter 12 | Education in China, Nanshan Foreign Language School |
| Chapter 13 | School trips and outings |
| Chapter 14 | Overseas Chinese complex and tourist attractions |
| Chapter 15 | The End of The Rainbow 2001 |
| Chapter 16 | The Pot of Gold (China's Future) |

# Introduction

As a primary teacher in London's Inner City for over twenty years, I was used to seeing children and their parents from all around the world. London is a multi-cultural city that blends its diverse population as best it can, with hundreds of different languages and dialects, exotic foods and different scripts. The schools are enlivened by such a colourful mix of different nationalities.

As a language specialist in three big London schools, I developed my own interest in learning languages and different cultures. I travelled as widely as possible during the school holidays and learnt Bengali, Arabic and Chinese. The holidays were never long enough. One year I spent in Russia, (as it was then known), following the silk route, through Tashkent, Uzbekistan to Alma Ata in the Tian Shan mountains.

As I sat in a beautifully decorated Yurt, the Nomads' circular structure centred by a huge wooden pole, I drank Kumiss, mare's milk and gazed spellbound at the high mountains. Over the other side lay China, a country to many shrouded in mystery for centuries. To me also a source of mystery and wonder. The nearest I had been was through teaching pupils from Hong Kong, and to various events in London's China Town in Gerrard Street.

We always celebrated the minorities' special festivals in school; the Spring Festival and Chinese New Year were no exception.

# Chapter 1

## First Visit to China 1987

On my first visit to China, I travelled alone to Beijing, to the famous 'People's University', in order to study Putonghua, the common speech of China used on TV and radio. The summer course lasted six weeks, I was just able to fit this time in during the school summer holidays.

## Beijing

It was very hot during that summer of 1987, and quite a culture shock. So many people, bicycles and traffic. Noise, pollution, different food and studying in order to make sense of things happening around. Days were long on the campus.

Many students went home for the long vacation, travelling all over China back to their families and home towns. Always some remained as they could not afford the rail or bus fares. Summer studies were held for Chinese and foreigners alike. In 1987, communication was looked upon with suspicion between Chinese and foreigners. Any visits to our dormitories had to be checked and visitors signed in and out.

Home visits were taboo. If any foreigners did manage to visit a Chinese family, everything was reported and double-checked.

## Life on the Campus

The 'People's University' is greatly respected by the Chinese people, it was built for them and they feel it belongs to them. It enables students from poorer families to have a chance to study at university level. The prestigious 'Baida University' further up the road is for top officials and Cadres offspring.

The dormitories, canteen and surrounding areas on the campus were basic by Western standards. I was on the top floor, and lucky enough to be given a room of my own, which also had a bathroom attached (this was used by a teacher during the term time). The room had a single bed draped by a necessary mosquito net, a fan on a floor stand, a desk, chair and wardrobe. On the desk was a large thermos which had to be filled with boiling water direct from taps on the ground floor. Cool drinking water had to be purchased at the many small stalls. The canteen, also on the ground floor, was large, the food served from a long hatch.

Breakfast was rice 'congee', a watery porridge made from rice, steamed bread buns, (like white rubber), yoghurt, hard boiled eggs and sponge cake. Milk or tea was available to drink. Lunch was rice, chopped veg and unidentifiable meat or fish. The same in the evening.

The breakfasts were passable, the rest left much to be desired for Western palates. This was remedied when the other students and I found the 'Friendship Hotel' and its bakery! Real fresh bread and good cakes. There was also a swimming pool and a regular Friday night film show for ex-pats in English and Chinese. (My husband and I came back in 1988 and made full use of these facilities, as we were in China for most of that year.)

That summer of 1987, my class, which was 'Intermediate Chinese', sweated and pounded our way through the tonnes of Oral Chinese, try valiantly to read the characters (it takes 4000 characters to read a newspaper). Homework was given daily. We worked from 8 a.m. to 12 p.m. In the afternoons we were free to study or visit places and practise what we had learnt, through travelling on buses, shopping, meals out and so on.

Six weeks is not long in which to study another language, but we could manage to get around and also had longer visits arranged for us. On our own we discovered the 'Summer Palace', and the 'Purple Bamboo Park', an area where the old men took their caged birds for a walk and airing. We visited tea chops, and watched older citizens perform Beijing Opera in outdoor spaces. During the early morning many people could be observed practising their exercises, Tai Qi Chua, Qi Gong, and rhythmic exercised according to age and inclination. I joined an early morning group on the campus to learn Tai Qi, the slow, sustained graceful movements which, combined with breathing techniques, gives a feeling of calm and tranquillity before the next onslaught of the day.

Arranged trips included an evening at the Beijing Opera, Acrobats, and of course, a visit to the Great Wall at Badling. On this trip we were taken to visit an old people's commune. They grew their own produce and had pumpkins, marrows, cucumbers, apples, many green vegetables, lettuce and tomatoes. Their little rooms were spotless with all items standing neatly to attention. They had leisure rooms in which to paint, do calligraphy, chat, smoke, and play cards or mah-jong. A simple, well-ordered life, they all seemed content.

The Great Wall is fantastic, 4000 li (mile) long, over mountains, through hundreds of small villages. Turreted square lookouts were set out at regular intervals. The ascent is very steep in parts, the scenery exhilarating, a mind-boggling achievement at the expense of many lives in the past of China's long history.

## Beijing weather, cycling, walking, clothes and shopping

The weather is always very hot and humid during a Beijing summer. My first introduction was to one of the hottest seasons for many years. People were sleeping out in the street on carts, on the floor spread-eagled on straw matting. Others sat in the shade of trees eating red juicy watermelon and spitting out the black pips. There was a festive feeling in the breathless air.

We cycled nearly everywhere, at least you could generate a small breeze for a while. We shopped in the cool of the evenings under the canopy of trees, for fruit, salad, vegetables and bread. This was a good chance to use our newly-acquired Chinese with the stall holders. Being small, I was able to buy some ready-made clothes. On the campus were some good tailors, I bought cheap but good quality silk and had some dresses made up. I am still wearing them today.

I got to know some of the Chinese families who lived and worked at the University. The tailor's family for example; they had a few rooms, one of which was used as a workshop. The grandmother had her own smaller room opposite and had a fine view of the customers with which to enliven her day. Each visit I could speak with her a little more in Chinese. The tailor's two small children would peep shyly into the room.

A large kindergarten was run for the workers' children, I cycled round to visit it several times. The children played outdoors a lot and had some good outdoor equipment, slides, sand pit, swings, pedal cars, bricks etc. They appeared happy and well looked after, although overcrowded like the primary schools they would next attend.

The social life on campus for our English-speaking group was modest. We played table tennis or ping pong as the Chinese students called it. We had some lively knockout matches. One hot night I stayed up and was the only foreigner left playing. I took on the kitchen staff, young men with attitude. I kept on winning, surprisingly as they were all good players, but I had been playing every day since arriving. In the end, the sheer heat and exhaustion beat me after my eighth opponent, a victory for women.

They were a good-natured lot of lads. When going out for the night they would lacquer their long hair, then fashionable, and wear Cuban heeled shoes, and suits with the name of the manufacturer on the sleeve, outside, so that all could see the maker's name and guess the price.

The girls were wearing see-through dresses, very short, with underslips attached that finished at thigh level. This ensemble was worn with knee or thigh-length stockings and high-heeled shoes. Hairstyles varied from waist-long, black, swinging manes to the New World image of short, sharp, boyish haircuts or perms, usually favoured by older women. The older generation could still be seen wearing the blue peasant-style suit and Mao cap.

A favourite evening occupation was a slow walk to the fountain in the centre of the garden grounds. This fountain sprayed different heights and levels of intensity to a background of music such as Strauss Waltzes, very cool, relaxing and welcome after the day's toil.

## Walking Styles

Beijingers have an unmistakable walk, a long loping but graceful gait. Maybe this is because such large distances have to be covered when walking. I noticed the different walks in other cities.

Shanghaiese are quicker and use smaller steps. Peasants in the city walk the same as in their home towns or villages, slower and unhurried or slightly bent and with a sideways, short step; these are the 'stick stick' people who are used to carrying heavy loads on the end of a bamboo pole across their shoulders.

In Wuhan, on the Yangtze River, the streets are packed, people wander across roads without looking, often knitting or reading as they walk. Too often there are traffic fatalities especially with young children.

I witnessed several road accidents in Beijing. The victim would lie in the road covered by a white sheet if dead, until the ambulance and public security had done the necessary measurements around the victim and cars or cycles involved. After they had all gone, the road was marked out with white chalk and cordoned off, the outline of the victim clearly marked.

Posters showing the dangers of road use were shown in prominent places, and for road education, graphic pictures showed the incorrect and correct way to walk, cycle and drive in the city, plus the consequences. Health posters were also prominently displayed in the same vein, against drug abuse and cigarette smoking, as yet largely ignored, as cigarettes are cheap and in China still give a macho image among young men. It is rare to see a woman smoke. This was fourteen years ago and things have changed for the better, especially in health care.

Cycling in Beijing was one of my main pleasures. You had to adjust to the rhythm and pace of the City and traffic. Cyclists appear to be going slowly, but you are blocked into a solid mass of workers, all busy coming and going. By maintaining a seemingly-unhurried pace you actually arrived at your destination quite quickly and always with life-long friends made on the way.

Hemmed in by four lane traffic, it was advisable to follow only the cycle paths, these were narrow, pleasantly cool and shaded by many trees. Sometimes the smells were bad from blocked drains and culverts of stagnant water.

People would talk to you as you rode along. It was another good way to practise my Chinese or in some cases their English. It led to many interesting meetings. Maybe an invitation to visit another college or to attend the popular English corners in local Parks. We all had our individual little adventures away from the campus.

I found a pleasant market area, very shady, I often stopped to do some sketching, this invariably drew large crowds of onlookers, which was unnerving and not conducive to good art. However, it was a good way to meet people of all ages. A group of children asked me to meet their parents. We went down a winding Hutong or lane to an earthen-floored, palm-roofed home. There was one room with a double bed for the parents, and a smaller room for the children and old couple. They were welcoming and charming in the generous style of peasant families the world over.

I gave some impromptu lessons in English in return and left a few sketches.

Further up the road I saw a sign with a painting of children dancing. I stopped and found myself outside a Children's Palace, this is the name of specially built weekend places of excellence for very bright pupils to develop their particular talents. They can do art, music, dancing, science etc. I sought permission to have a look around and spoke to the teachers. They had some very interesting projects in progress and were industrious and lively.

The purchasing of a bicycle was quite involved. Luckily one student knew the ropes from an earlier visit. We travelled down town by bus, the long double bus, concertinaed in the middle by a squeeze-box of rubber, known locally as 'Gong Gong Chi Che', the 'che' being the word used when describing any form of transport. You could put the correct amount in a box on entry or pay a conductor. These buses were always packed, you would be lucky to get a small wooden slat seat for the hour-long journey.

We finally arrived and looked at some cycle stores, our group wandered around choosing from exotic names such as the Phoenix, The Flying Pigeon to well-known brands such as Raleigh and Gresham Flyer. I choose a sturdy maroon Flying Pigeon and paid around the value of twenty-five pounds in FEC, Foreign Exchange Money. We then each had to have our chosen steed tightened up and saddles adjusted etc, there were around twelve of us plus our Chinese teacher and foreign affairs leader. Next we had to cycle to the Public Security Bureau to be officially registered, just like a car in England. Again it was a lengthy business with so many of us at once. We had to produce passports, visas, photos and fill in numerous forms, all outside in the hot sun. When the paperwork was complete each bicycle was given a metal number plate, this was fixed by metal plates.

Finally, exhausted by the experience, heat and hunger, we had to pedal the long distance back to the University.

Special areas were available on the Campus for pumping up cycle tyres. If you needed further repairs there were many roadside cycle menders who gave excellent service for a few fen.

As the daughter of a racing cyclist and cycle shop owner, I came to appreciate their services under the most basic circumstances. These roadside services included mending umbrellas, shoes, broken zips, watches, just about anything which we would today in the West throw away as unusable. Fourteen years later these roadside menders are still around, and form a useful backbone to many people, especially those with low wages.

You sit on a low stool and wait for your shoes etc, to be repaired. It is inspirational to watch a craftsman at work, usually the older generation.

# Chapter 2

## Teachers and Students

My classmates came from England, Canada, and Japan. The Japanese students were all in an advanced class, having the advantage of eastern culture, and similar writing in calligraphic form, a simplified version taken originally from the Chinese script. We got used to meeting them in the dining room, at social outings etc, but they were segregated from us by their leader. They had different outings and separate coaches. The Japanese organisation was a marvel. At the slightest hint of rain the leader would sit the students down and issue them all with an umbrella, or if sunny, check their headgear.

The girls were giggly, flirty and dramatic. They would posture and pout, lean on a boy they liked, even pretend to faint in the heat to get attention from the boy of their choice. The boys of course showed off, stripping down to skinny vests, posturing in heavyweight poses and play boxing with each other, but they were diligent students, polite even though distant with our group. Some longer trips we did travel together, for example, on a weekend excursion organised by the University by train, northwards to visit Datong the home of steam trains, where the great engines were built. Our group was taken to the factory to see the making of these steam engines and to actually ride on one. But true to form, the Japanese group were siphoned off on arrival and taken to visit some famous flying sculptures, there was no choice.

On arrival at the factory, we were escorted into a large

meeting room and seated around an oval table. China mugs of tea with lids were available for each person, as at most functions. Various managers and engineers then gave us a potted history of the making of these giant engines. We were all presented with a handsome red, silk-covered book containing a certificate with places for our name, date of visit and to testify to the fact we had pulled the whistle on the working steam engine.

Next we were shown around the huge workshops, where individual parts of the engine were made and assembled. The safety factors left much to be desired but with so many people available for the Chinese workforce, these details do not seem so important to them as they do in the West. We saw a very near miss, with a large object driven on a wire at great speed knocking off the small helmet of a worker. What if he had not been wearing any headgear? Many did not bother.

Our visit was most informative and enjoyable, especially the ride on the footplate of a working engine where we got to blow the whistle!

The hotel where we stayed was of a high standard, what a contrast to our simple dormitories and all the more enjoyable for the contrast. After our evening meal, some of us went to the hotel disco. It was fun, but after such a full day, I soon went to bed.

Datong itself seemed a poor area; it was black everywhere from the coal dust used for the engines. The housing we saw was basic hutong living, the people curious and friendly. I saw one young man, black with coal dust from head to toe, lying on the pavement fast asleep in the heat of the day. He looked like an exhausted miner. I took photos of a little boy who was proudly wearing a small version of a PLA soldier's uniform, complete with hat and gun. He was around three years old.

Several of our group bought complete sets of ex-PLA

uniforms as gifts, also military caps and badges.

## Friends

The other students on our six-week course came from all walks of life. I remember them all with affection. We had a common aim, i.e. to learn as much Chinese as possible in six weeks and to experience a new culture. You quickly bond when you are together in the same situation. Our levels of expertise in Chinese were sorted into three groups, basic beginners, Intermediate and Advanced. I had studied for a term at the London Language Poly, so tried the intermediate. In the beginners' class you, were drilled on the four basic tones which underpin Putonghua. Grammar was also heavily on the agenda. I had a reasonably good vocabulary so tried the next stage. This also involved not just reading Pinyin, the written form with which we are all familiar, but the actual Chinese characters. Slowly shop and road signs began to make sense, the wonderful voyage of discovery that a child learning to read experiences when words take on meaning.

It was hard work, not least because none of us were used to such humidity and heat. There were no fans in the classrooms and the hours were long. We had one morning break where we charged into a student's dormitory and made drinks and exchanged news. I often wonder what happened to those classmate friends. I will not name them in case of any embarrassment it may cause.

I remember one tall, thin boy who became our best student. He ran for miles each morning before breakfast. The Chinese would offer him food on his return. He returned to study at Oxford.

Another young man was a college lecturer. He used to cycle around with me and another student. He was the only European good enough to be in the Advanced class with the Japanese students.

Another was fluent in Cantonese, he had a pretty Chinese girlfriend. Another London-based young man, connected with a famous theatre, became an excellent local guide for us all. The girls were like me, there for the language and culture. At the end of the course we gave a performance for the staff and Chinese students. Some of our group did cross talk, the Chinese comedy acting, others sang or danced, played the guitar and ukulele, and one memorably did roller disco. A versatile group indeed!

The Japanese students were among the audience.

# Chapter 3

## Teachers and Further Travels

Our Chinese teachers were two women. One, called Sanfunjia Loashi, was around forty years of age. A traditionally trained teacher, she was good. Keen and friendly, she taught with only a few words of English. By the time the course ended she knew as much English as we had learnt Chinese. The second teacher for our Intermediate class was in her twenties and my private name for her was Pippa Longstocking. I don't recall her Christian name. I could not understand a word she said and all her lessons were long explanations about grammar. She wore short skirts and long white stockings, hence my nickname for her.

I learnt a lot from my first teacher, next to nothing with the second. As I had already concentrated hard for two hours before the second teacher began, this may have had something to do with it. The teachers always accompanied us on any outings. They had given up their holiday in order to teach us during their summer vacation so were entitled to some fun.

I shared a bedroom with Sanfunja Laoshi on the trip to Datong. A little uncomfortable at this close proximity, I could not help but observe the various undergarments she wore, as she slept in her vest and knickers. These were of the heavy duty kind, more useful for army exercises in the field. I wore some more feminine silk pyjamas, she was equally fascinated. They were made in Hong Kong.

An unfortunate incident occurred. A teacher from

another group came to our room. The two teachers spoke together and kept glancing across at me. After a while my teacher said that her friend wanted me to change some of my Chinese money and give her some foreign exchange currency. FEC could buy things that Chinese money could not. I felt trapped into the situation and exchanged a small amount, albeit unwillingly. It was not a pleasant atmosphere. After this exchange, my teacher left the room and joined her friend, leaving me thankfully to sleep on my own.

She did not return again, except to collect her luggage in the morning.

I know the teachers were poorly paid, but I did not appreciate the underhand way of dealing. This idea that all foreigners are rich continued throughout my years of working in China. Today many teachers in the South of China have more money and a higher standard of living than some Westerners.

Thankfully, the system of FEC was abolished in 1994.

At the end of one month, the other two weeks were for travelling to different parts of China, still with the group. Most of us continued together.

I stayed behind in Beijing for a few extra days, then bought an air ticket to rejoin the group in Hangzhou, a beautiful area of Eastern China, not far from Shanghai.

If it was hot in Beijing, it was unbelievable in Hangzhou. It must have been forty degrees centigrade, or more, plus high humidity. The difference was that we were not studying, although still conversing in Chinese whenever possible. We were out in the country in a low white hotel building, set in a Chinese tropical wonderland of lakes, streams, rustic bridges, bamboo thickets of various species, small wooden huts, cork pathways and huge black and emerald green butterflies. It was an enchanted place. Ten minutes walk away was the famous

West Lake, beloved by poets and romantics. Here you could hire a long boat with a canvas cover overhead to shield you from the sun. The boatman rowed or rather punted using a long pole. There were many large carp waiting eagerly near the surface for titbits thrown by visitors. Pleasant tea houses surrounded the edges around the lake.

In the centre of the lake were small islands. One student and I visited the Island of the Moon. We disembarked and sat in a tranquil tea house. The book title 'Tea House of the August Moon', sprang to my mind, but it was still July! To add to the dream-like quality of the island were Chinese people, dressed as if still in the Qing dynasty. Our waitress wore a long flowing robe of pink and blue, with wide sleeves and sash. A little piece of time that stood still. We made our way back to the waiting boatman under willow trees, through moon gates, the circular shape depicting a full moon.

On another day, it was stormy. The lake with its deep purple mountain backdrop took on a menacing quality. The boatmen had difficulty in reaching the other side shore in safety. When it rains, it is torrential. The lotus leaves and flowers bend to accept the weight of the raindrops. When the storm is over everything gently steams and the frogs continue to croak. The cicadas rustle and sing as the sun beats down, drying their wings. Ice cream sellers open up their hand-pushed carts and look for likely custom.

A large international hotel welcomed us into their lounge while we had tea and got a taxi back to our own hotel, named after a flower.

Hangzhou is famous for its silk industry; I visited the town only once as we were some distance away. It was large and noisy. Following some directions from a waitress where I had lunch, I found myself for a brief minute in a men's sauna. I don't know who was the more surprised.

That must have kept the gossips going for a while, the day a blonde walked into the men's sauna! Walking around alone you got to meet people in a way different from being with a group. People were more likely to engage you in interesting conversation without fear of being overheard.

This was not a time to be outspoken.

## Suzhou

From Hangzhou our group travelled to Suzhou, a little place full of enchanting gardens. These gardens were built in the time of the Emperors. Small, intricately pebbled paths led us down through plants, flowers and shrubs of an infinite variety. Undercover pathways had fan-shaped open windows from which to observe the garden as from a picture frame, moon shaped doorways led to yet another scene. The master craftsmen, architects and garden designers of a bygone age live on through the gardens of Suzhou.

## Shanghai

Our next stop was a visit to Shanghai. We travelled by coach from Suzhou. This time we were staying at the Music Conservatory. It was very similar to the University accommodation in Beijing.

We passed many small practise rooms with individual pupils playing different instruments, piano, violin, oboe, flute, traditional Chinese instruments, and singing.

This time my room mate was one of the Japanese girls. She spent much time in packing up gifts to send to her family. Each item was beautifully done.

I went with two students to post some mail and a parcel. My first experience with the bureaucracy of the PO. First we had to find a shop which sold boxes, paper, sticky tape and string, none were available at the PO. We returned and did up our parcels, only to have to open them again for the contents to be examined before writing each item in triplicate on some forms. There were separate counters for each transaction, all with a crowd of people waiting, shoving, pushing, the concept of a queue does not exist in China. After weighing, we were waved to another counter, where we had to purchase a length of white cloth, borrow a needle and thread and sew our boxes into a tight jacket. This took most of the day. As I was due to visit the house of one of the music students, I got worried about keeping her and her family waiting.

The Post Office was near the waterfront known as The Bund. Nearby was the famous Peace Hotel, which used to have great jazz sessions in the days of the French and British colonials living in Shanghai. The French influence is still to be seen in the architecture. The lifestyle is much more relaxed than other parts of China and the people speak out more freely.

I met my friend, who waited at the college for me. We got a bus to her parents' home. They lived in a wooden-fronted house with big rooms full of old style Chinese furniture.

The mother was very interested in British literature and knew authors such as the Bronte's, Shakespeare, George Eliot, etc. As a fan of the latter I promised to send her one she had not read. On my return to UK I sent her a copy of "Eliot's Romola", plus Bronte's "Wuthering Heights". I did not have to sew up this parcel.

My new friend's family had prepared a small banquet for lunch, the food was very good. The father was an ex-university professor. He and his wife were now retired. Their daughter was a staunch Christian and ran around organising meetings. I never discuss religion in a Communist country, so kept to music and literature. It was a pleasant experience to enter a Chinese home. I also met their neighbours and was asked if I would take a letter and some money to give to their daughter, who was studying in London at the Royal College of Music. Later I met their daughter at Covent Garden for a meal and to deliver their package.

Many such incidents happened. Once at my London home, a friend brought round a Chinese student. He turned out to be a close friend of the girl who befriended me in Shanghai, also a musician.

Shanghai is a vibrant, fast-moving city with cosmopolitan ideas. The smartly-dressed traffic police direct the traffic from high, circular stands in the centre of the road. At festivals people pile the stands up with gifts for their hard-working traffic police. Not an enviable job, standing in the heat, noise and pollution for hours on end. Shanghai was our last call before the flight home, via Hong Kong.

# Chapter 4

## Return to Beijing

It was to be another year before I returned to China. I had to finish teaching at my school in Westminster and allow time for injections, visas etc.

This time my husband and I were travelling together on our own itinerary. I was very keen to cycle as much as possible. We made our base in Beijing at the People's University, with which we were already familiar. From here we were able to leave most of our belongings safely for several weeks at a time and travel light. To begin with we cycled around Beijing and on the outskirts further a field, to get adjusted to the Chinese rhythms and language again.

It was like a homecoming, the sights, smells and sounds from the previous year firmly entrenched on my mind.

We shopped at local markets, and I cooked on a calor gas stove out in the corridor.

The Beijing food is bland, but their tomatoes are big and firm, ideal for a cool summer salad. The Beijingers slice them and sprinkle sugar on their tomatoes, not to everyone's taste!

The Western restaurants in the big hotels were excellent; we ate at the 'The Jiango Greenery', the 'Beijing Toronto', the 'Holiday Inn', and the 'Shangriala' Hotels. What we saved on our limited budget by staying at the University meant that we could afford to splash out occasionally, at least while we stayed in Beijing. We cycled out to the mountains called the Fragrant Hills, quite a long ride there and back in one day plus climbing the mountains. The mountains are famous for the wonderful red leaves of many Canadian Maple trees in the autumn.

The student leader at the Campus became a good friend and often accompanied us on our cycle trips. On one visit to the Fragrant Hills, I heard sounds I recognised as a country wedding. I detoured from the main road and sure enough found a village wedding in full swing. My husband and our friend came looking for me and within minutes we had all been invited to attend the wedding as guests. The bride was in the traditional red wedding dress and the groom smart in his outfit. They gave us drinks, sweets and cake. I took some photos, they had no camera with which to take pictures. In the following days we cycled back to the small village with a set of memories for the young couple. They were at work when we called, so I left them with a neighbour. It was a happy, spontaneous event.

Our student friend, who I will call Lu, although not his real name, taught us to play Chinese chess and took us to meet his family. It was a long cycle ride at night, no cycles use lights in China, so we bowled along the cycle paths hoping to avoid obstacles. Many manhole covers are either left off, or stolen, they are lethal big holes; many accidents must occur.

At Lu's home, his parents made us very welcome. His father was the ex-curator of the Palace Museum, know in the West as the 'Forbidden City'. His mother, an ex-teacher, made us a good meal before we had to cycle the long distance back to the Campus.

One Sunday we were taken to visit the Summer Palace by Chinese friends. They took us to a restaurant where many delicacies were made exactly as they had been in the days of the Dowager Empress, wonderful choux pastry creations like swans or lilies.

We were then escorted to the big lake and given a ride in a motor boat which Queen Elizabeth and the Duke of Edinburgh had used the previous week. It was not for the general public's use, but our friend's uncle was the manager of the Summer Palace. We were fortunate indeed. The boat was moored at an island in the middle of the lake; here we entered a lovely, small Ming Dynasty building for refreshments. An ideal hideaway for visiting dignitaries for which it was intended. The day was very hot, but here isolated on the lake, it was cool and peaceful.

A day of memories like a necklace of pearls and jade.

It is often the little things that remain in the memory: the smile of a stall holder; the old woman who made exquisite handmade baby's shoes; the cries of the Hawberry hawker, selling his fruits coated in toffee from a back-pack to school children; the toddlers running about in their split pants, no potty training needed here; the smell of jasmine and the Yulan blossoms; the harsh, strident voices of peasant women; the mournful hoot of steamers and ferries on the great rivers; the never-ending drills and earth-pounding machines for endless buildings for an endless population.

Many challenges have to be faced when travelling without a group or unit. We surmounted many hurdles in order to travel by train. First the station, then the ticket, simple, but not in China. The station in summer is packed, ticket queues up to weeks long. Humanity waiting to move. Families camped on the station, outside the station, some with tickets but no train for days. Our only way was to buy our ticket with FEC and soft class rather than hard class. The prices were a little more, but all the rail prices to us were cheap. Our next problem was to find the platform from where the trains left. I felt so stupid, running around using my limited Chinese, asking where was the platform was for Xian, or where did the trains go from. We could not see any platforms or trains anywhere.

Suddenly a large iron gate was opened and the crowd charged. We were swept along and then found a maze of different platforms with incomprehensible Chinese names. Finally we recognised Xian on the side of a large, snorting green and yellow engine with high carriages. Each carriage had its own attendant, a fierce-looking woman took charge of us and kept our tickets for the entire journey until we reached our destination.

Our carriage was clean, nicely covered with white cotton covers. Our companions were a PLA officer and a TV director. The journey was long and interesting. We had good conversation, part English, part Chinese. We ate in the dining car, and were glad to leave as the tables were covered all over with food from previous occupants. We had the usual rice, veg and bits, covered with soy sauce, with plenty of hot water for tea. Most passengers brought their own tea and mug with a lid or a glass jar. We had bought tin mugs with lids.

The passing scenes were glimpses into the lives of countless Chinese, mostly through the countryside and mountain areas. Bright green paddy fields of rice with figures in blue tops and pants wearing big straw hats. Riding home at night along narrow earth-packed lanes to little villages of tine or wooden homes, some with bamboo thatch roofs. I saw banana trees, bamboo thickets, vegetable plots, pigs, geese and poultry farms, sometimes oxen pulling crude ploughs. A never-ending, fascinating variety of life.

Glimpses of the Great Wall, the Yellow River and huge bridges afforded excitement and pleasure to many passengers. Our soft class compartment had four bunks ready made up. The people in hard class also had bunks in rows of four but with no privacy, as they stretched down the full length of each corridor. The toilets were the usual hole in the floor, the length of journey not improving them. I slept quite well through the night.

We finally arrived in Xian. From a travel agency in Beijing we had booked a modest hotel on the outskirts of the city. No other foreigners were in this hotel or surrounding area. They made special cakes for our breakfast instead of the usual rice congee. We hired bicycles everywhere we stayed rather than take our own on trains.

Cycling into Xian was like entering York city with its big city walls. We passed through big gates to enter inside this vibrant, walled city. The noise, bustle, colour and teeming mass of people could be over whelming at times. We found the famous landmarks named the Bell and the Goose Pagodas.

We drank a weak beer at pavement cafes, it was still very hot and liquid intake is very important. Another day we took a small tour bus to see the famed Terra Cotta Warriors. It was quite some miles from the city centre. On the way we stopped at the Bampo Park. This had delightful gardens in the old style, leading to a house where the Nationalist leader Chiang Kai Shek was finally captured by the Communists, prior to the founding of the People's Republic of China. We looked at the small museum and historical photographs, then were taken to see an early life-size model village of the Bampos. These people were a matriarchal society.

Our small group of about eight people continued to the site of the warriors. Inside a huge construction we looked down at the hundreds of warriors, each one with a different face. It was disappointing not to be able to get close or be allowed to take your own photos. These could be bought at a souvenir shop. These amazing warriors are still being excavated today. They have brought many tourists from around the world.

Arriving back, we went for a drink at a hotel and found a Tang Dynasty concert was being performed. We sat at the front and had a good view of the graceful dances, traditionally played instruments and gently flowing robes of bygone times. We then cycled back through the city gates to our modest hotel.

We decided to continue our journey to Chengdu in Sichuan Province. Again by train. Another long overnight journey followed. You need to be healthy and relaxed to travel in China, there are many frustrations and patience is the best way when dealing with bureaucrats. For example, on being told there were no tickets to Chengdu for a week, we went and sat down for an hour. I then reapplied to another ticket office and was successful in obtaining our two tickets. Never believe everything you are told.

# Chapter 5

## Tibet

'Eagles soar undauntingly on high, under the blue and vaulted sky'.

On arrival at Chengdu we decided to stay at a bigger hotel, after our long journeys and basic accommodation we felt in need of some luxury. A very good move as it turned out. We were to need all our strength for the next stage of our travel. The hotel was big and had the American Embassy in its grounds.

It was hot, full of beggars outside the hotel gates, and teeming with hundreds of people waiting outside the railway station for the trains which may come today or next week.

We treated ourselves to a Sichuan dinner. Sichuan cooking is the opposite to the bland food of Beijing, it is famous for its fiery, hot dishes. I had some wonderful spicy king prawns. I also decided to have my hair trimmed and washed at the hairdressers, I was given an excellent shoulder massage along with the hair wash.

Fully restored, we called at the hotel's travel agency, which advertised trips to Tibet. Knowing how difficult it was for foreigners to get permission we were not really expecting success, however the fact that we were students at the People's University gave us some special immunity. We could travel the next morning.

Tibet

Another milestone and dream come true. We arrived at 5 a.m. for the early flight. Huge monks, wearing gold and maroon one-shouldered robes, strode past. The plane was small, the mountains below sheer and pointed, a tremendous vista stretching for miles. After a four-hour flight we arrived at Gonggar airport, a large field surrounded by purple mountains, a rushing river and a few Tibetans waving placards.

We were met by a driver and guide for the eighty-mile journey to Lhasa. It turned out to be a sightseeing tour for the first forty miles. We stopped on the roadside to look at a huge colourful Buddha figure carved into the rock face, according to the local people it suddenly appeared one night. Our next stop was a small temple, which we were told was the foundation of Buddhism, the religion having been brought over by a monk from India. We entered the well-tended gardens accompanied by the guide, a small dog and a monk. Inside the gloom were Tibetan thankas, pictures of gods and myths depicting stories of the fight between good and evil. We passed rows of chanting monks, and through incensed-filled rooms, golden butter-lamps burning in front of the gold statue of Buddha.

The rest of the journey passed in a daze as our guide told us about the history of Tibet. It had been a long day.

The countryside took on an ethereal quality which I felt all the time we were in Tibet. The sky seemed so low and near, the landscape wide and open, yet always surrounded by high mountains. The full, rushing river ran alongside us all the way, sometimes we could see small circular coracles at the water's edge. These were boats made from yak skins stretched over a wooden framework. Occasionally we passed small homes. The Tibetan house has a flat roof and each corner which leans in at right angles has tall coloured prayer flags flying in the breeze. The white houses have bands of strong colour around them in shades of ochre yellow, red and dark blue.

Small, very confident watchdogs with curly tails appear along the road, they can be fierce. On the roofs I could see barley grain and corn cobs drying. The basic diet is tsampla, barley grain rolled into a doughy consistency and tea mixed with yak butter.

We arrived at our small Tibetan-run hotel called the 'Sunlight'. We were the only foreigners.

I stayed outside in the warm sun, feeling very fit, almost euphoric; the guide came up and urged me to go and rest. He recognised what I did not, the first onset of altitude sickness. I walked upstairs to our room and collapsed in a heap outside the door. Luckily our guide was following and watching, he must have had previous encounters with other guests.

Rest is very important for a couple of days to acclimatise, especially after entry to Tibet by plane. The sudden changes in altitude are too abrupt. Entry via Nepal or India on walking expedition is safer, but we had entered from the Chinese side.

## Politics and Religion

Tibet is an autonomous region belonging to China. It has always caused a lot of controversy in the world. It is a landlocked place of mystery, which for many years has been isolated through its geographical position. The religious fervour of different sects of Buddhism, with its spiritual leader the Dalai Lama, also lends inspiration to devotees, poets, artists, writers and photographers around the world.

On the other hand it whips up Western sentiments on human rights of political prisoners and the so-called injustices done by the Chinese.

Firstly, Tibet has had would-be invaders for centuries, including the British. Looking back through history, it is easy to forget the good things which China has achieved. The times of feudal law in Tibet were horrific. Families were not allowed to own their land, their taxes were so high they had to slave for ever to pay off debts, sell or give their sons and daughters into serfdom, and have their limbs chopped off randomly.

After the initial, sad smashing of temples and holy places at the time of the Cultural Revolution and the exit of the Dalai Lama to India, China began to help Tibet to build roads, hospitals, a university at Lhasa, and schools and better health care for all. Internal politics are not the affairs of the West. If they must intervene, let them also balance the picture, by looking at some of the positive aspects that have been achieved in Tibet. Outbreaks of violence which occur and are reported in the world press are usually begun at special holy festivals when more visitors are around. Who starts these actions? Usually the monks themselves, in many cases ex-prisoners for violent deeds. It would be naïve to assume that everything is wonderful for all Tibetans today. There is poverty still, but many own their own small holdings, can buy better goods and children can study in schools. Most families own a yak, which provides wool for spinning and making into cloth for clothes, bags, etc. They labour in the fields, have milk and meat when needed. Dogs, pigs and chickens scratch around the earth.

The culture of Tibet is unique, so too is the culture of the many other ethnic minorities throughout China, such as Yunnan province, the Mao, Yao, Guangdongese, Xingjiang etc. Different costumes, music, songs and dances and languages keep alive the spirit of each area.

The Tibetan script is beautiful to look at; many

priceless manuscripts are still being discovered today. Many more were ransacked and stolen by other countries at the times of occupation and turn up in Western Museums for preservation.

## Potala Palace

The first view of a building seen in photographs and read about frequently is amazing. The reality is in front of your eyes but has a dreamlike quality. So it was when I first saw the Potala Palace, residence and spiritual retreat for Buddhist monks and leaders. It rises up smoothly, like a white wedding cake, with sheer sides and countless long narrow windows. To reach it you must climb a very steep hill, pass through massive gates and then climb endless vertical ladders inside the Potala itself to get from one floor to the other.

I entered alone. It was dark, lit only by hundreds of yak butter lamps. Many rooms led off from each other into one main room. Each held sculptures and paintings of deities. Some were fearsome warrior-like creatures with green purple or yellow demonic faces. Others showed Buddha's with benevolent expressions, sometimes serene, others laughing; each representing the forces of good and evil – the continuing cycle of birth and rebirth.

Gold and silver objects glittered in the gloom. White 'khatags', thin white scarves hung everywhere. These are given to guests and hung around their necks as a mark of respect and peace. A few monks glided quietly around, but the place seemed oddly deserted, it was an eerie experience. Each room had its own special deity and history; all had lamps and incense burning their sweet pungent fumes. The semi-dark, combined with the pervading smell of yak butter lamps and lack of air, all contributed to a slightly sinister feeling. I had climbed many high ladders, been steeped in Buddhist history and lost all sense of time and reality. It was time to go.

Coming back down to the huge wooden gates, I saw with dismay that they were closed and heavily padlocked. Here I was in a place the Mecca of thousands of people, and I couldn't wait to get out! Eventually a large monk appeared and, without a word, opened a small gate set just inside the main one. He pointed to the sky. Around the sun were many rings of colour, a nimbus of light. This, I was later informed, was a special omen. I was just glad to be on the outside, having looked in. I was especially happy as I felt I had achieved an ambition for my brother Steven who has long been fascinated with Tibet. The spirituality of the place is heavy, what else lies behind those walls to give such a feeling of menace as well as awe, I wonder.

## Holiday Inn, Norbu Linka Park, a farm and school

We had now acclimatised to the thin mountain air. It even affects the Tibetans at times. Pregnant women are sent lower down to give birth in a local hospital. Most women and children have very high-coloured cheeks, the men tend to be brown and weather beaten. Feeling fit and free of headaches, we had arranged visits according to our choice. I chose a farm and school for my visits. I was keen to see ordinary, daily routines. On the way we passed the newly-built Holiday Inn Hotel. How was it able to pay its way? Very few tourists were allowed into Tibet and most were backpackers from Nepal or India. We met only one small group of tourists who were tightly scheduled and only allowed to stay in Tibet for three days.

We had already been there for ten days.

Inside the hotel (we had to look!) it was cool and air conditioned. A notice board inside the lobby held messages for mountain climbers and people who may have made it to Tibet, followed by medical advise. A small shop sold postcards and embroidered Buddha wall hangings. We had lunch in their pleasant restaurant with its canopies of blue and white.

My husband tried a yakburger, the meat was chunky and declared fine. As a vegetarian, I had a salad with crème caramel. It was strange to see a Western hotel in the middle of a deserted Tibetan plain. Our own small hotel, entirely run by locals, was much more homely and cheaper. My husband bought extra burgers for our guide and driver, who would not come to the restaurant with us, no doubt they needed a rest too. They were delighted with the yakburgers.

Country school visit

Out in the countryside, away from Lhasa, the mountains seemed very close to our ribbon of winding road. Finally we came to a little country primary school. Within the long wooden hut were two classrooms, outside a concrete playground. The headmaster and teachers were very welcoming. The children chanted their lessons in sing-song voices. They were dressed in warm clothes and woolly hats. I watched a maths lesson and writing lesson using the Tibetan script. They also learnt Chinese (Mandarin or Putonghua as it is now called), the common Chinese speech as used on radio and television throughout China.

Not all Tibetan children were so lucky to have schooling in those days, although education today is now law for all school-age children in China. Country children the world over have always been needed to help work in the fields.

Tibetans are forever smiling, laughing and singing. The peasant workers travel to work loaded together in big open trucks, others walk or cycle. Tibetans, Han Chinese, and ethnic minorities mix, live and work together. We met some charming families and individuals. Some of our hotel staff doubled up at night to perform Tibetan folk songs and dances. This took place in the dining hall, which was a separate building to the sleeping area.

The girls wore dresses with extended long sleeves which are used a lot during the dances. The gown opens off-centre to the right and is tied around the waist with a colourful silk sash. The material is a woollen cloth called 'phula'. The girls' hair was braided into more than a hundred tiny plaits interwoven with coloured silks. The men wore white, red or green shirts under their gowns. Often the right arm is free from the sleeve in hot weather or sometimes both sleeves, which are then tied around their waists. The front part of the gowns is lifted at the front to form a pouch in which a purse can be placed to carry small things.

The folk dances were circular or in line formations, with simple steps accompanied by singing. Tibetan instruments were used throughout, locally made and twangy to my ears! However, it made an interesting evening.

## Shopping in Barkhor Square

Our travel budget was tight, we had little money to spare after the flight and hotel bills, but I couldn't leave without some souvenirs from the Roof of the World.

I bought two small prayer wheels, woodblocked Tibetan script prayers wrapped in yellow and red cloth, and a few necklaces or coral and turquoise. The ethnic, winged hats were tempting, with their rich gold-embroidered borders, but I resisted.

Around the square itself were all manner of activities

and enough colour for a Hollywood movie. Monks from the yellow hat sect, monks from the red hat sect, their cockscomb distinctive headgear rising above their serious, weather-beaten wise faces, praying and chanting, sitting in groups or singly, totally absorbed.

People twirled prayer wheels as they circumnavigated the Jokhang temple three times. Old people wrapped in ragged clothes were lying on the pavements, small dogs ran in and out playing with children. Chinese soldiers in Mao caps and blue uniforms bought cheap cigarettes and cakes, others sat outside pavement cafes with soft drinks or 'chang', gingke fermented barley beer and the ever-popular buttered tea.

The tall good-looking Khampas from the eastern part of Tibet, the Amdo region, were selling their decorated knives and daggers. They are known as Tibetan warriors, a tall, proud and brave people. They wear their long, black hair in a roll, wrapped around with red cloth. Around their waists hang curved daggers, and they stride around in boots with the long gait of mountain people.

We visited the sacred Jokhang Temple by invitation from a young monk, who spoke some English. The building is distinctive with its golden wheel and two deer sculptures on the rooftop.

In front of the temple, pilgrims who had travelled for many miles, measuring their body length along each step of the way, were now doing full body prostrations over and over again in order to gain merit in the next world. They had wooden boards on their hands and knees. We followed the young monk into a large sunny courtyard, where novices were engaged in vigorous spring cleaning. Further inside the building the same activities were taking place, shaking of mats, sweeping, polishing, filling the butter lamps and picking up the ankle-deep money dropped by visitors towards the temple's upkeep. It was a hive of industry with a pleasant atmosphere.

Our young guide was a merry soul with a winning smile, the Buddhist faith certainly appears to make for a happy people. They believe that they come back to Earth many times in different forms before they reach 'Nirvana' (spiritual eternity and unity of the highest order), portrayed as the jewel in the crown, the symbol is the Lotus blossoms. This flowering plant rises above the water with its roots below, hence the allusion to Heaven and Earth.

Many people twirl prayer wheels as they walk along. Inside are tightly rolled-up mantras in Tibetan script. The rotation of these wheels is said to bring peace throughout the world.

I reckon a lot of twirling needs to be done!

We visited a tea shop in the square. We sat upstairs on the balcony of a two-storey, wooden building, a good way to absorb the minutiae of teeming life below.

Walking back from the square to our hotel, I observed some well-kept typical Tibetan houses, pretty with window boxes full of flowers, the white walls contrasting with the red, yellow and blue awnings. A day to take out of my memories and savour in future years.

Norbu Linka Park is the Summer Palace of the Dalai Lama. He left from this palace and travelled secretly in March 1959 to India. A group of Khampa resistance fighters accompanied him on the long march. Travelling through the night, they reached Indian territory on the Assama frontier. Since then Tibet's spiritual leader has not returned. He left at the age of twenty-four years. His rooms are still furnished and include his bathroom on view to the public. There are many beautiful paintings and thankas (wall hangings) and the audience room, complete with throne. The rooms are large and airy with a mixture of simple and more elaborate, carved furniture.

As we progressed from room to room, a Tibetan

family were also visiting. They were utterly overcome at being in the presence of the Dalai Lama's treasures, genuine love and awe shone from their eyes. Their belief is touching in its sincerity, to them the Dalai Lama is a God King. Everywhere we went, people would stop and ask us for photos of his Holiness.

Tibet has been under attack from the outside world over many years. Britain invaded the south-eastern coastal areas of China in the 1840s and tried to separate Tibet from China in 1913, where it convened a conference at Simla, hoping to divide Tibet into an inner region, which would belong to China, and the other half to be autonomous, which Britain hoped to dominate.

Today the whole of Tibet is called an autonomous region and is part of China.

The gardens are Norbulinka were cool and pleasant. So much history has passed through these gates in land-locked Tibet, it is difficult to imagine the flight of Dalai Lama and his followers and the battles that have been fought to preserve the unique culture and religion of this area. Battles still continue in small settlements throughout the world, from, 'Free Tibet' campaigns and marches for freedom groups in USA, UK and Europe, mostly by people who have never set foot inside Tibet and probably never will.

Culture is handed down through the generations by each ethnic group, from grandparent to grandchild, father and mother to sons and daughters. I doubt that anything will destroy the Tibetan culture and beliefs. Tibet inspires dreams, hopes and mystery. In thoughtful mood, we carried on to visit a farm.

My first experience of butter tea was at a small farm holding that we visited. The farmer and his wife, sister-in-law and small boss-eyed son shyly welcomed us. Inside the low, long, white farmhouse was a large room with a wooden floor and a central pole running up to the ceiling. The furniture including the Tibetan carved and painted chest and sideboard, tables and chairs were of simple bamboo. They slept on wooden settles, covered with brightly-coloured woven blankets.

We were invited to drink buttered tea. I was delighted with the offer, I didn't want to leave Tibet without sampling the tea and 'Tsampa'. I was given both. The tea tasted like a watery broth which coated the back of my throat, probably a good protection against the cold and changes of temperature, but in all honesty it must be an acquired taste! Tsampa is like a heavy dough, chewy but palatable helped by a drink. I made polite noises.

I sketch a lot and did some quick drawings of the lovely heirloom chest and the little boy. It is a useful way to give instant gifts. Outside we were shown the animals; the family yak, they are big, hairy animals, quite gentle like a big cow with extra long horns. They had goats, pigs and poultry. In the courtyard was also the farmer's 'Chang' making machine, the weak fermented beer made from barley. They also grew a few vegetables in the sparse soil. The women spun wool, dyed it and made cloth. They were self-sufficient, but it did not look an easy life.

The scenery around was magnificent, purple mountains spilling down to the edge of the narrow white road. Patches of green up the mountain sides and above, the deep, blue sky and odd, fleecy, cream clouds.

Another day we observed the Drepung Monastery which is outside but not far from Lhasa. This is a practising monastery, full of monks in their distinctive maroon and gold one-shouldered robes. Our altitude sickness prevented a trip on the river in a coracle as planned, time was passing. Many Tibetans would wander into our hotel room, and watch us, sitting quietly on the floor or trying to converse with us. We were able to communicate a little in Putonghua. They were so full of fun and zest for life.

One day, earlier in the trip, my husband collapsed. A huge, strong, young fellow, who was with us at the time, carried him across his back, as if he were a child, and he is no lightweight. He went to the Tibetan hospital and was hooked up to some oxygen and a drip. We were both travel-weary. You need to be healthy to travel around for any length of time in other countries and different cultures. This applies to any age group. In Tibet, it is advisable to drink plenty of water to avoid headaches.

It took me nearly a week to acclimatise. If you are a visitor for three days only it can be a traumatic experience, not to be recommended for anyone with heart or respiratory problems.

Before we left I arranged a banquet to thank the people who had help us. About twenty of us sat around a circular table – the hotel manager, his staff, guide /interpreter, driver and nurses etc. We were a merry throng with no political or language barriers. The food was beautifully presented.

The next morning we set off on the eighty-kilometre journey back to Gonggar airport. At Gonggar there were no facilities and we were not allowed into the airport building until the plane arrived. It was sixteen hours late! A whole day and we could go nowhere as there was no indication of when it would arrive.

I made friends with two ragged children and we sat in the dust playing five stones and drawing pictures with sticks in the ground. Groups of other passengers, Chinese and Tibetans, played cards or chess, slapping down the cards noisily and generally having a good time.

I wandered a little way along a riverbank and saw a young woman washing her waist-long, black hair in the water. Scores of small children were leaping in and out of the river, swimming like fishes. Later some school children came out of a nearby school, singing the lessons they had learnt that day. High-cheeked, rosy faces and laughing eyes.

I later used the two children at the airport as an inspiration for an illustrated children's book. I called it 'Yusi and Tashi in Tibet', followed by another called 'Children of China'.

The plane finally arrived and we were hurried aboard. We landed in Chengdu and were told in some agitation by the air hostesses to evacuate the plane immediately, all hand luggage to be left behind. The panic was created by an extra case being found on board and no passenger. All our big cases were dumped onto the tarmac and examined. Later we reboarded and were on our way back to Beijing.

# Chapter 6

## Beijing and Beidahe

Back on the campus, it was hard to settle down again after our long journey. I was doing some research for a magazine in the UK on 'Children's Games in China'. I settled down to a spell of writing and local study. It was a time of very hot and humid weather.

After a few weeks we decided to leave for a cooler climate.

Soon we were back on the train to the seaside resort of Beidahe, a few hours journey from Beijing and the summer residence of top Chinese officials.

Beidahe, on the East coast, was a delight – cool sea breezes, safe bathing and nature reserves for wildfowl. There were long, wooded lanes for cycling. We hired ours as usual from where we stayed. Cycles could be left safely for a few fen (pence), with an old man or woman, who sat under shady arbours watching hundreds of cycles in special stands. A variety of locks exist for bikes. Mine was a clip affair permanently attached to the back wheel with its numbered key lock system.

We swooped up and down hills, along the coastal paths and down to the local market selling shells, clothes, swimwear, fruit and ice-cream. Ice-cream carts were everywhere. The goods were all packed with dry ice. You could buy a variety of ice-cream in cones or ice lollies. The vendors would shout their wares, 'Bingiling, binguaaaw, (ice-cream/ice lollies).

The town further on had pleasant tea shops to refresh

us before the return journey. We could have green tea, very healthy, red tea, black tea – the strongest, or delicate jasmine tea and many other varieties. I enjoyed jasmine, a delicate pale amber liquid, all drunk without milk or sugar.

We ate local crab with 'striped potatoes', these turned out to be chips! We visited a disco; it was full of young men and women dancing alone, in front of mirrors, a great place for show-offs. We played table tennis, lawn tennis, and bowling, cycled and swam in the sea. It was a much-needed restful period.

Travel does broaden the mind, lighten your pocket and fulfil many dreams. It can also be very tiring both physically and mentally. You need to be healthy, patient and flexible. You have to deal with bureaucracy in another language, follow their rules or at least try to understand them. Tiredness can make you irritable. Knowing when to stop is important. Meeting other Europeans can be either a) very welcoming or b) intrusive, depending on where you are and your state of mind.

During our travels we hardly ever met other foreigners, apart from the intensive six-week course at the People's University.

Distances are vast in Beijing. Our university, located in Haidan district, was an hour's bus ride into Tiananmen Square and near the shopping area of Wangfujin Street. We cycled down frequently and visited two 'Friendship Stores', one for foreigners who used FEC (foreign exchange certificates) and one for Chinese, where you could use the local money called renmimbi.

Whilst in Beijing we visited the Temple of Heavenly Peace and its beautiful garden park, Beihai Park, for a wonderful lantern festival at night, also Purple Bamboo Park where they held weekend 'English corners' for Chinese and foreigners to meet and learn English. Many friendships were made in this way.

Another favourite was Bird Park, where older, retired men would take out their caged birds for an airing. They hung these bamboo cages on the trees. Some cages were left covered, to enable the younger birds to listen to a leader bird singer and then, when the covers were removed, the young birds would imitate the sweet songs of the leaders! They were wild birds such as thrushes, linnets also minah birds. These were caught and sold in markets. The old men looked after them very well, although they should have been free. The cages were large with lovely porcelain water and seed pots. As the men walked, they swung the cages to and fro, so the bird's had to grip hard with their claws. This was to provide exercise and strengthen the birds!

We cycled to the 'Summer Palace' many times and visited the Forbidden City known to the Chinese as The Palace Museum. I climbed to the top of Coalhill Park which is set high on the top of a steep hill overlooking the whole of Beijing.

We saw the seasons change, from spring with its young green willow trees lining the canal and river banks, to the cherry blossom trees in the parks. Then came the difficult days of dust storms. Sand blown in from the Gobi Desert covered everything; if you needed to go out during these days, you had to tie scarves around your mouth and watch your eyes. Summer brought many tropical flowers. Many big watermelons were piled up to sell whole or in big, juicy slices. Autumn was delightful for the red Japanese maple trees flaming up the sides of the Fragrant Mountains. Winter was bitter, with snow and biting winds from Siberia.

Our nearest hotel was called The Friendship Hotel or Youyi Binguan. It had a coffee lounge, where ex-pats and students could meet and have a cheap meal. The dining room was splendid, the waitresess wore the long split to the thigh silk cheosams, but the service was terrible. It was renowned for its poor performance and rude waitresses, but we still enjoyed going. The atmosphere was great. There was also a roof garden for beer etc. There was a bakery in the grounds, an outdoor swimming pool and regular Friday night film shows in English and Chinese. We frequented a Russian restaurant near the zoo, halfway to Tiannamen Square. Today everywhere is full of MacDonalds, Kentucky Chicken restaurants and pizza parlours. We were there for the opening of Beijing's first-ever MacDonalds, I had a strawberry ice-cream! The best bargains for short stay visitors are still silk clothing and cashmere garments. Some side streets near the big hotels sell the best silk.

The luxury life of hotel meals and living soon palls. We returned to England after an excellent year away.

Macdonald's are everywhere!

Rainbow Room.

Animal Snap in any language! (2001)

A Chinese business lunch following interviews for a top Managerial position on the Science & Industry Park. English Interviews taken by Mr James Moffet (top middle) & myself. (2001)

Clever ice-sculptures for Valentines Day. Kuala Lumpur Hotel: 'Palace of the Golden Horses'.

At the top of yet another mountain on English/Chinese teachers and staff outing for school leaders. <u>Front LHS</u>: Director Li. <u>Front RHS</u>: Dean of Middle School, Mrs Zhang. <u>Back Row in cap</u>: Headmaster Mr Wu, (my 2<sup>nd</sup> Headmaster).

Attending the school's opening flag ceremony (NFLS) (1995).

Presentation of velvet embossed scroll for 2<sup>nd</sup> place in dance /aerobics team from Shenzhen Nanshan Foreign Language School.

Nanshan Foreign Language School (1999).

Mr Hai Ping Gong, Education Inspector for Nanshan Education
Bureau and Jiangsu Province Schools, his wife, daughter Jenny
and Karim, where we were guests for a week.

A visit to a clever student of English just out of hospital
following a fall on his head, holding my book for Chinese
Young Students (Jiangsu Province).

Mr Guo – Deputy & Acting Headmaster & Jacqueline on
Leaders Weekend boat-trip to mountains (Guangdong).

Karim and Jacqueline with Secretary at Shenzhen Special Zone
Daily Nanshan Readers Club where we gave lectures.

# Chapter 7

## VSO, UNDP, Wuhan

We had been travelling, researching and living Chinese style for some years. I felt it was time to put our knowledge of teaching language and communication skills to good use.

I answered an advertisement for the United Nations Development Programme, who were looking for volunteers to work in different parts of the world. I went down to the VSO (Voluntary Services Overseas) at Putney Bridge in London for a day-long interview. Young people were there applying via VSO, to go to Romania, Africa or wherever their skills were most needed. The tests were quite tough. For application to UNDP you need a degree and a qualification in the area with which you hoped to help some third world country, plus a commitment to stay for two years.

After a wait of around six weeks, I was told I had been successful and would I like to teach English to Post-Graduate Doctors and Surgeons at a College of Traditional Medicine in Wuhan, Central China. My husband was accompanying me and was to find work later.

We were now plunged into a world of visas, medical checks, insurances, paperwork, a veritable whirl of activity. You have to remember so many things, such as the redirection of the mail, cancelling any orders in the UK, what to do with your house and car, telephone, gas, electric and so on. Family and friends begin to call more and more, you feel like you are never returning.

In our case we were away for a total of fourteen years but always returned to the UK once or twice a year.

We flew to Beijing first for briefing with the UNDP officer. This gave us time to get over the jet lag, before the second flight to Wuhan on the Yangtze river.

As with most schools and colleges, the term commenced in September (1991/1993). Coming down over the Wuhan area, the plane flying low, it looked like a huge series of lakes stretching for miles, with only tiny strips of green between them.

We arrived at the airport, which was yet another field. Waiting for us at the exit were three figures, the Head of the College and two young Chinese English teachers. We were welcomed and whisked away by car several miles to Wuhan. Accommodation had been assured for us both, by letter from the College to the UNDP representative in Beijing. The head however expressed surprise that there were two of us. A new building was being erected and was not ready, so we were moved into a hostel belonging to the college and within its grounds. We had one bedroom, an ancient bathroom with wonky shower and hole-in-the-floor toilet, plus a shared kitchen.

The Hubei College of Traditional Chinese Medicine was originally built by American missionaries, and had some pleasant, old-style buildings, some with original, tiled, curved roofs, other ordinary concrete-block structures housed the students' dormitories.

The college was founded in 1959. It has an area of 201,960m, which includes the campus, herbal garden and the pharmaceutical factory, a total area of some 65,503m. The Chinese love to measure floor space, and sell apartments and housing according to floor area, rather than room numbers as we do.

I loved the trees and plants. My favourite was a magnolia (yulan) tree, with huge, creamy-white blossoms and the rare ginko biloba tree, whose medicinal properties have now been acknowledged by the West as an aid to memory retention, used for Alzheimer's Disease.

There are three departments, including six sections. Students can study for an MA in TCM (seven years) and for a BA degree (five years), Orthopaedics and Traumatology BA (five years), Traditional Pharmacy BA (four years), Chinese medical nursing (three years).

Whilst I was there, they had fifty-eight teaching departments and research offices, plus forty-one laboratories. A college library houses a total of 250,000 books, of which 100,000 volumes are TCM books, many are rare editions.

I found some of these books invaluable for my study of Traditional Medicinal plants and their uses. Although written in Chinese, I was able to study the Latin names and compiled a list with a doctor student of mine. This was later published using the English, Latin and Chinese names for each plant and diagnosis.

My students, all post-graduates, were a mixed, lively group, eager to learn and improve their English skills. Visitors came from all over the globe to visit the large teaching hospital affiliated to the College. It was necessary for the doctors to communicate in English. They had been given text books to bring into class. We looked at these briefly but mostly used oral English, via games and conversational topics. Each student was encouraged to speak for as long as possible. We began with impromptu talks of two minutes each. Over the two years, most of the students could hold their own, and an audience, for a good hour. Several of my students got scholarships to study abroad. We then turned to practical English topics such as 'At the Airport', 'Customs and Culture in the West', 'Food', etc. Some students went to Canada, USA, UK or Scandinavia.

Before leaving I arranged for each student to feel what it was like to dress in an Islamic state. We all had a lot of fun together. My husband sat in on many of my classes and one day we all went on an outdoor English class. This was greatly enjoyed. We walked through the long market area next door to the college, discussing the produce, prices, etc, and of course taking photographs. Another had a tape recorder to play back 'sounds' and 'voices' at a later date.

We travelled by bus down to the Yangtze River, about ten minutes ride along a very busy road.

All simple activities, but the students had little spare time in their busy days and nights (when on duty), so enjoyed this more relaxed approach. Their use of English was creditable.

We had several parties, to celebrate a success, Christmas, New Year, Spring Festival. Everyone brought something to share, pumpkin seeds were a great favourite, black and white. We had fruit, sweets, drinks, biscuits, the classrooms were decorated and the games played were simple but fun. Music and dancing completed our entertainment. Chinese people in some parts of China have few, if any, luxuries. These highly-skilled people were earning a pittance compared with the West, but they were happy to be doing a useful job to help others. It took very little to given them something to enjoy. Their pleasure came from doing things together.

Another time I took them back to our apartment – we finally acquired one in December – where I showed them how to mix and make pancakes as it was Shrove Tuesday. I had to use a wok, but I tossed the pancakes well. We had an enjoyable time, eating pancakes and drinking coffee, oh yes, and learning English.

The students helped us to move our belongings to a newly-built apartment in time for Christmas. We had plenty of space, a living room, study, two bedrooms, bathroom, dining area and small kitchen. It was furnished well enough. We had a fridge and washing machine, real luxury items in those days.

A small balcony led off from our bedroom. Here we hung out washing, using a long bamboo pole to put the clothes up on to an extended arm for drying. Below were the gardens of the ground floor people, we were on the first floor. These gardens were pretty and practical. They grew grape arbours to keep cool, Wuhan is very hot and humid in summer, up to forty degrees centigrade. Flowers were grown in old tins, any handy container; the ground was left to grow vegetables, marrows, beans, onions, carrots and turnips. The garden below kept chickens and one garden had a small dog and a rabbit. Rats ran in looking for chicken feed, they came from the nearby market.

The market was colourful and sold veg and fruit, tofu (bean curd), eggs sweets, spices, shoes and clothes, toys and household goods. Live poultry, fish, frogs, eels and snakes were also sold. We could buy fruit and vegetables including Toudou (potatoes), but no bread. Many things which we ate in the West were not available, especially dairy produce.

China is a great slimming place, or at least it was, nowadays you can buy most foods in cities. As I am small and only weighed seven stone on arrival, I didn't want to lose too much. After two years in Wuhan, I was down to nearly six stone. We seemed to eat a good diet, but all those hidden fats in pastry, cakes and freezer meals as found in the West, were unavailable, not even a MacDonalds in those days! There was a canteen on the campus but it meant getting no rest from talking to students between lectures, so we ate at home.

I cooked on a calor-gas, two-ring burner, mostly with

a wok. We also had an electric kettle which heated water then kept it warm all day, very useful, and an electric rice cooker. This big pot cooked rice to perfection, we added raisons for a pudding. The bottle of calor gas cost us thirty Yuan (about £3 a month). Later when living at Shenzhen we found we had been misled by the college, the gas should have lasted much longer.

Walking daily through the market place was not a place for the squeamish. Live produce such as hens or ducks were weighed on scales and dumped unceremoniously into string bags, Eels, snakes and frogs were gutted on the spot. Skinned frogs were threaded onto bamboo skewers reading for cooking.

Wuhan is famous for its variety of river fish, these are prepared with ginger and garlic.

Fruits included exotic lychees, star fruit, mangoes, breadfruit, local bananas, melons, huge apples, grapes and many types of oranges. Vegetables included corn, courgettes, onions, carrots, lotus root, bamboo shoots and many other local greens.

Several stalls sold a large variety of tofu (bean curd), from pure white, quivering blocks to firm, mottled brown or blue varieties. We bought groceries from small shops such as honey, tea and instant coffee. No butter or cheese. We purchased eggs from a cheerful stallholder, these were always unwashed and had to be scrubbed before cooking. The market place got very muddy, plastic shoes were necessary, but it had its own character and special ambience.

The heat and long hours would cause violent arguments between either customer and stallholder or rival stalls, arguments that become public viewing for all. A crowd would gather and join in, each taking turns to berate or shout encouragement. Some were nasty, choppers would fly and victims finish up in the nearby hospital. It was as well to keep moving in these circumstances. These were all peasant folk, who had walked for miles in the early hours to set up their stalls each day, then sat patiently in the heat for hours before packing up in the early evening to return home. No wonder that they sometimes lost their cool. Their takings can't have been much either.

We got to know many of these cheerful peasants. One old lady made exquisite, tiny, embroidered, children's soft shoes (buxie) I bought several pairs as souvenirs. Vendors shouted their wares, some sold long sticks full of hawberries coated in toffee, and others made popcorn in an ingenious machine which exploded when ready!

Another man made wonderful, thin, toffee patterns onto greased paper, in the shape of animals, birds or flowers, each a work of art, and eaten in two seconds by rosy-cheeked children.

Further up the market, a crowd gathered around to watch one artistic individual making vases and fancy holders from old tin cans. Machinists sat outside their stalls full of silks. You chose a pattern from a book, they measured you up on the spot, and made your dress or shirt etc, within hours. Cost around UK £1.00. Shopping in Wuhan was cheap and fun.

One of the most famous landmarks in Wuhan is the Yellow Crane Tower. This is a tall pagoda which you can walk around on the inside and outside balconies. Many dynasties ago, this was the place where scholars of note and poets, would pace up and down to gain inspiration for their intellectual offerings. The tower can be seen from many places in Wuhan. It has an orangey-yellow tiled roof and ornate carvings of animals and birds around the building. The roof has the upturned wings which are so Chinese-looking. From many of these upturned, winged roofs hang wind chimes or bells. It is a relaxing and calming sound to hear the sound of bells as you stand viewing much of Wuhan and the River Yangtze below.

Any popular viewing place in China is a signal for Chinese families to go there at the weekends, cameras in hand. Children are posed beside sculptures or flower gardens, on rustic bridges overlooking golden carp or just standing to attention with the rest of the family in stiff poses.

Below the Yellow Crane building, which is approached via many steps upwards, are well kept gardens. Here you can sit in the shade under centuries-old trees. One tree, known as the Shaking Tree, had a group around it looking up. One person gently scratched the tree trunk and the whole of the tree began to tremble, from the top leaves down to the bottom branches.

Trees are something which we greatly appreciated down the main shopping roads. We travelled again on our newly-acquired bicycles. In summer, Wuhan is extremely hot and humid. They trees are trained to bend over the road from each side. The made a cool canopy through which to cycle.

Wuhan is in the centre of China on the Yangtze River, halfway between Beijing and Guangzhou, and is the capital of Hubei Province. A busy rail centre connects two of China's important cities, and boats leave daily to either Chongqing (upstream for five days) or downstream to Nanjing and Shanghai (two days). The population of Hubei is approximately 54.39 million; Wuhan is comprised of three cities, Hankou, Hanyan and Wuchang, the latter being where we lived. Regular ferries cross the Yangtze daily from one side to the other. Sometimes we would cycle from the college, secure our bicycles and cross on the ferry to look around Hanyan, or Hankou.

One of the longest bridges in China crosses the river. It is a double bridge, with traffic and pedestrians crossing. It is manned by police at regular intervals. In earlier times, during a revolutionary uprising, the bridge had been taken over by students, this will not happen again.

My living expenses were paid into a bank in Hankou by the UNDP monthly. We were taken by college car once a month over this long bridge in order to collect some cash, it usually took all morning. The Bank of China in Hankou was a wonderful affair of glass and chrome, big desks and swivel chairs, but the tellers didn't want to know their customers. They would sit away from the counters, chatting, filing their nails, laughing, looking at new magazines, anything but work. Since those days there has been a big shake up of many industries, computers of course changing the face of many work places.

Before 1994, the money for foreigners was still in FEC, this had to be changed into local money, remnimbi, in order to shop locally. Black market touts could be found in many areas. We had been taken for a ride many times during our first year, and decided to take advantage of the system. Outside the Yangtze Hotel in Handou we had found a small baker, real bread at last! We were approached one day by a furtive looking individual inside the shop and offered a monetary exchange. It was a good deal which enabled us to have a slap up meal at the hotel, for free. We carried on this system once a month.

I cannot leave Wuhan without mentioning other local beauty spots, notably East Lake and Wuhan University grounds. East Lake is where many families and lovers meet at weekends. It is a cross between a landscaped park, to a more natural environment around the big East Lake. Here you can ride pedal boats shaped like ducks or swans, go in rowing boats or motor boats. Small fairground attractions cater for others. Eating never stops, from Hot Yam stalls to barbequed kebabs, ice-cream and lollies, hot and cold drinks, crisps, biscuits and fruit. Others bring their own picnics.

The Chinese have grown taller and fatter between the years of 1987 to 2001. Better living conditions, more spare money and the habit of snacking between meals has also led to obesity in many school-age children. As the policy in China is for one child families, most children have two proud sets of grandparents to spoil the one chick in the nest. The choicest morsels from plates are popped into the mouths of toddlers from chopsticks of parents, grandparents and friends. They look delightful with their big heads and plump floppy limbs when still in split pants but not so great when they reach primary and middle school.

Chinese babies are carried around until they are at least three years old. The ground is dirty or unhygienic, the weather is too hot, humid, or windy, wet or cold. They are kept indoors until around 5 o'clock in summer to avoid the excessive heat.

As they progress to kindergarten, they again have everything done for them. On entry into primary school they have the rude awakening of having to fend for themselves. Many at the age of six or seven years cannot do up their own buttons or shoes. Children are kept young for as long as possible, which in turn keeps down the age of burgeoning puberty and sexuality. Teenage life is another story! But classmates forge strong links within the same sex, and are to be seen in many parts of China, girl and girl, boy and boy, hand in hand or with arms around each other. The peer pressure is greater than in the West, the links formed last for a lifetime and are stronger in most cases than eventual marriages, the age of marriage being mid-twenties.

We saw little in the way of romance between couples, and marriages, often arranged by families, were undertaken more as a duty. Many married couples were separated via their work units, each forging strong links which included going to numerous banquets, dancing, drinking and socialising after work. If the leaders arranged it, they had to go. The same with working abroad. One partner of a couple would take off for foreign parts without much thought for the partner or family left behind. This is often a permanent arrangement, if one person gets an extended visa and work permit. Even within China, husband and wife can be separated for thousands of miles for years because their work unit has moved them. We saw this happen with one of my doctors. He had a full time job at the hospital and looked after his five-year-old daughter alone. Luckily there was a kindergarten within the college for workers' children. His wife, also a doctor, was delighted to leave them all and go to study in Canada for three years, her daughter was devastated.

China expects and demands allegiance to the flag and Motherland. Loosening the family ties strengthens the commitment to country and socialism. Everything is done together, never alone.

## Traditional Chinese Medicine

Traditional Chinese medicine has a history going back 2000 years. Herbal medicines were used in conjunction with heat, such as wrapping bark around hot stones, by our early ancestors. These were found to relieve or eliminate symptoms of diseases.

Later therapies were devised using hot, medicated compresses and moxibustion. This is a mixture of traditional Chinese herbs, mixed according to the need, often Chinese mugwort leaves, and placed inside a cylindrical-shaped tube of card, which is ignited at one end. The resulting fumes are placed near an appropriate acupuncture point near the body but not touching the skin, in order for the vapours to penetrate quickly. The patient feels a gentle warmth and quick pain relief. Several treatments usually clear up most complains and it is a popular, therapeutic technique.

Cupping is another heat-induced way of finding, pinpointing and relieving backache, sciatica, and internal troubles. This involves the placing of small glass cups, which have been warmed around the rim, into position onto the bare skin. When the cups are removed some time later, the resulting skin leaves red circles, which appear to the onlooker as burns; they are in fact created by the flow of blood, which has been drawn to the surface of the patient's skin, highlighting the afflicted areas and allowing the practitioner to further advise his patient and to give healing and pain relief.

It was found by accident that pain in one part of the body would be eased when some other part was pricked. Treatment followed, using Bianshi stone needles, these were followed by bone needles. Gradually acupuncture came into being and the therapy of Channels was born.

Eastern healing techniques have gained rapidly in the UK since my two years in Wuhan. Today it is quite common to visit a hospital and be referred to an alternative practitioner or medicine. Up and down the country are medicinal herbal shops with clinics attached. They advertise acupuncture, aromatherapy, shiatsu, traditional Chinese massage, reflexology, (foot massage) etc. In the West, our grandparents knew the value of medicinal herbs and flowers, many would be gathered in the countryside and used in cooking, and to make medicinal concoctions and poultices. Overcrowded doctors' waiting rooms, often for trivial complaints, were overcome to some extent through health education. The NHS issued many leaflets on how to cope with various illnesses, symptoms to look out for and advice on what to do or who to contact. In short the population of Britain was taught to treat its own simple ailments.

In today's stressed society most people want reassurance through face to face consultations, many pay for expensive counselling. Yesterday's society had a different structure – mothers stayed at home, grandparents lived close by, families were large and there would be someone with a sympathetic ear. Today families often live many miles apart through economic and other reasons.

The same thing is happening in China. High-rise blocks of apartments re-house some of the older members, they lose their daily contact with neighbours. Where once they could sit at ground level on their low bamboo stools, gossiping and chopping vegetables for the mid-day meal, plus looking after one grandchild, now they are confined to a lonely existence.

In our teachers' block live several Chinese families together. They have little room and live on the highest floors, with no such luxuries as lifts. One old lady had serious heart trouble and had to live apart from her husband for nearly a year following an operation. She needed a lower apartment so had to live with another family miles away. Her husband was still teaching, although at retirement age.

Two other grandmothers looked after young toddlers, their patience was sorely tried in these cramped living conditions. Children were not taken out during the heat of the day, only from around 5 p.m., keeping a lively toddler amused alone was not easy for them. In return they lived free with their son or daughter. They will be freer when the toddlers go to kindergarten from around three or four years old. There are plenty of private kindergartens but too expensive for many people.

Healing Herbs

Over many years, Taoists closely studied the healing composition of herbs and became highly proficient in the use of plants.

Surgeons could anesthetise their patients for up to six hours, without side effects, just by using a herb tea. This some six thousand years ago! They even removed organs from patients and washed them in a herbal solution before replacing, but this was realised not to be the answer, the final analysis lay in illness prevention.

The ancient doctors and surgeons saw that illnesses were the result of a particular lifestyle, that constant surgery could not prevent the recurrence of a tumour, whereas a change in lifestyle could.

The Academy of Sciences estimates that there are around one million plant varieties in the world, modern science has not yet discovered all the properties that exist in herbs.

The Taoists call herbs The Forgotten Food. Our regular food gives only temporary strength but various plants such as ginseng can impart great vitality. (Ginseng must be balanced with other herbs when eating.) Ginseng is available as a tea, a pill, a plant to make your own tea.

Chinese health also takes into account the medicinal value of certain foods and divides tastes into sweet, sour, bitter and salty. They also take heed of the time of year and change in climate. Traditional Chinese medicine is a fascinating study and needs a book of its own, plus the will to follow and study all the complexities.

## Healthy living is a way of life

From early morning exercises to daily eye exercises in the classroom, the Chinese are taught health awareness from an early age. It is a way of life. Most school children know the rudiments of traditional Chinese medicine and health care. They grow up in an atmosphere of self-help and reliance upon themselves for the healthy functioning of their body and mind.

This includes the knowledge of Chi, which is the breath and essence of the life force. They learn how to breathe correctly alongside their daily exercises, similar to Yoga which is now enthusiastically practised in the West.

Qi Gong is another health-giving martial art. Those who learn this correctly and practise diligently can cure many illnesses and become physically strong.

On television I have watched many new exercises over the years, some using special apparatus such as huge balls on which to lie and move around, others with stepping stools, or strong, pliable, stretching ropes, light weights, even the western dance aerobics and salsa. Boys and girls alike wear the latest fashions, the more modern ideas of the West being a target for the younger generation, whilst we in turn benefit from their knowledge of the traditional Chinese martial arts and exercises.

Harmony with Nature

The Chinese people have always lived in harmony with nature. As long ago as the eighth century .a.d., the poet WangWei wrote "Look in the perfumes of flowers and nature for peace of mind and joy of life". Painters of nature were strongly influenced by Taoist ideas. The seasons are represented by flowers, trees and other plants. The Taoist cult of immortality is depicted as the narcissus flower, peach, bamboo, pine tree and the crane. They are the symbols of longevity and are to be found in the book Chieh Tzu Yuan.

Painters and poets try to interweave the ideas of the harmony of Yang (Heaven) and Yin (Earth) into their paintings and poetry.

The dragon is a symbol of the power of heaven and of analogous ideas. In Chinese work on Materia Medica (Herbal Medicine), the Pen T'sao Kang Mu, it is described as having resemblance to nine other creatures. Certainly animals rate highly in mythical tales, and many Tai Chi exercises are also based on animal and bird movements. The dragon appears in the sky, rivers and sea; he is associated with water and is announced by thunder and clouds. The dragon represents the power of restraint. The orchid, chrysanthemum, bamboo and plum tree are called the four gentlemen, symbolising various qualities of the ideal man, cultured, of good character and pleasing personality.

The Yang and Yin symbol is in every aspect of the Chinese way of life. Mountains (Shan) are associated with Yang, and water (Shui) with Yin. The harmony of this concept is evident in Chinese landscape painting and of trees and flowers in particular.

## The Mighty Yangtze River

The Yangtze flows beneath my feet, yellow, red and brown. Verdant-clothed hills rise sheer into the soft grey clouds, boats pass by, fishers, coal carriers, life on the riverside. Children run along the stony bank offering their smiles. The adults watch unsmiling, this is their world, washing, carrying, selling, sleeping. The slow unhurried life – while the Yangtze slips swiftly by.

# Chapter 8

## Cycles, traffic, exercise and an accident

Cycling was always a somewhat hazardous occupation, the traffic in cities being overcrowded, noisy and unpredictable.

In Beijing we followed the many cycle paths, excellent in theory except that cyclists often rode on the wrong side. Sometimes small cars, carts and animals thought it also their right of way. Open drains were another hazard. Man holes were left uncovered, apparently the value of an iron cover making them easy picking for thieves. We saw people who had bad accidents by dropping suddenly into one of these holes, especially at night. Cycles do not use lights in the dark in China, bad enough on a cycle lane but lethal on the open road. Along the roadside in Beijing in those early years, cycles had right of way over cars, not any more. Cars, buses, taxies and lorries totally outnumber the cycles. There were sit-up-and-beg style cycles for sedate riders with a shopping basket in front, tricycles with whole families draped across every available space, and my favourite sight, a grandmother sitting upright under her umbrella on a cart being towed by her son on his cycle.

Other traffic hazards included mules pulling coal bricks or long sticks, overloaded bikes full of flat, card boxes for recycling, and rubbish collectors, who wandered along the roads sweeping, spearing up rubbish and sorting it into separate bins.

In Wuhan we cycled on cycle paths where available but had to join the main road at intersections and junctions.

Down the main street, which was full of shops, we bowled merrily along to the strains of the latest pop music issuing from many stalls. The shady trees affording a pleasant shade in the heat and humidity. The temperature in Wuhan can reach over forty degrees centigrade (100f). It is known as one of the three ovens of China. By contrast, in winter we experienced snow and ten degrees below zero. During our first winter we had no heating of any kind. Heating is not used in China below a certain geographical point. Wuhan being halfway down the map just came into the area of no heat. The market stall holders and small open pavement cafes would light fires in oil drums, fed by coal bricks and wood. On these, they cooked meals and kept warm. The building where I taught my students was an ice block of concrete. The doctors had their own ways of keeping their circulation moving whilst sitting. They flexed different parts of their bodies at intervals and kept a ripple of movement going up and down their leg and body muscles. At break times I put on music and we danced to keep warm.

All work places have set times to perform morning exercises. These are arranged according to age. Young pupils in school have simple exercises to music, set by PE teachers in Beijing. These are increased and expanded for older middle school students. They are carefully graded and include the use of every part of the body. Sedentary workers, factory workers, middle-aged people and the older generation all do their own set of exercises. Young people do vigorous work-outs such as Wushu, (Sword Play) and karate, all ages to Tai Qi Chuan (slow, graceful, extended movements to create harmony between body and mind). Others practise Qi Gong, another form of mind relaxation, breathing and set stances.

One evening after work we cycled to a hotel some distance away to try and find a Western meal. At the hotel called the Lijiang was the Red Rose restaurant. The food was passable, the waitresses charming and as usual wanting to learn and practise their English. We had a pleasant evening and cycled back through the gathering twilight, our eyes by now accustomed to the dark road and all the dangers. Just as we approached the hill leading up to the College, a heavy tricycle lost control and ploughed straight into me, knocking me off my bike and onto the back of my head. The back wheels were a centimetre from going over my chest. A crowd gathered in the usual noisy Chinese way, shouting, gesticulating until the public security officer arrived to assess the damage. The young man whose brakes had failed was stricken; I later heard that he had been heavily fined. He didn't look as if he could afford a fen (penny). Also later, the road at the corner was widened to avoid further accidents of which there had been quite a lot.

My husband took me to the gatekeeper's hut where I was treated for shock. Later I was taken to the hospital and kept there for a week for observation, in case of head or internal injuries.

I learnt a lot about Chinese family life during my enforced rest. I was in the intensive care ward, which had two other patients. One was a lady dying of cancer, her son and daughter were with her daily. They both lived and worked in other Provinces but had made arrangements that one or the other would always be there. It is the custom for families to bring in meals for the patients. Meals are available from the hospital kitchens but as everything costs money, most people prefer to have home cooking, it makes the family feel wanted and involved.

The family do many menial jobs, which releases the nurses to do other work. Parents, aunts, uncles, etc, will cheerfully empty chamber pots for those not allowed to get up. Privacy is in short supply but in a mixed ward, when a woman wants privacy the men must leave the ward for a while, and vice versa. The other occupant was a man, who had just had a lobotomy (brain surgery). After a few days he was smiling broadly, it was good to see.

I had a huge number of visitors until the staff had to limit them. My students were all working at the hospital so I had plenty of company. The girls came to give me a body wash and have a chat. Another nurse got me to give her English lessons and asked me many questions. I found out later that this was to check I had suffered no loss of memory. After tests proved I was fine, I couldn't understand why I was being kept in the hospital. It turned out that my blood group was unknown in China, (Rhesus Neg. A.) Luckily I did not need a transfusion.

I was smothered by these kind, low-paid students with fruit etc. my husband did a sterling job in daily visiting as well as his own classes at the Nurses' College. He even cooked meals and brought them in a covered tin container.

During our second year it was my turn to visit him. Overcome by the heat and high humidity one day in the market he collapsed. Luckily we were near the hospital and a nurse and I managed to transport him, via a wooden cart, up to the main entrance. He was put on a drip and cooled down until his breathing had assumed normality. One of my doctor students, Steve, stayed with him throughout the first night in case he suffered from a stroke. They are very caring in their treatment. The hospital would be frowned upon from the hygienic point of view in the West, but they had all the necessary up-to-date life-saving equipment. The hospital trained their staff in both Western and traditional Chinese medicine. The best of both worlds.

## Ballet classes and a Kindergarten

As an ex-ballet dancer and head of my own dancing school in the UK, it was not long before some students in their early twenties asked if I would teach them ballet, my answer being, 'You find some more students and a place to dance and we can begin'.

We finished up in a large classroom of the kindergarten belonging to the college. After the evening meal, we would meet up and walk over to the kindergarten on the far side of the campus.

There were about ten girls and at one stage one boy. My husband was our music man, he played the tapes, stopped and started them as and when required. We began with barre work using the back of small chairs, centre work and adage followed. The girls were all graceful, most of them having done Chinese style dancing in their primary school years. It was hot work, still being summer, hot, sticky and humid. I began some dance sequences with them, to the gentle piano strains of Richard Clayderman. Now whenever I hear the music I am transported back to the kindergarten classroom. We even tackled the quick dance from Swan Lake, 'The Dance of the Little Swans'. Our young man who joined us had done ballet before and was very promising, but the strain of partnering ten females became too much for him.

My husband and I both enjoy ballroom dancing, especially Latin American. We were invited to many evenings which included dancing. The Chinese style of ballroom dancing is different, the rhythms stepped to a different beat. I could follow with a good partner, but it felt strange. In turn the students would try to follow the western style. We taught them some popular dances of the time, line dances, cha cha cha, etc.

For special events we were asked to perform a party

piece. My husband would play a ukulele banjo and sing along to the strains of George Formby, while I would do some ballet and international style dancing. The Chinese are surprisingly good singers and never lose an opportunity to have a karaoke evening. All teachers are expected to contribute and make their own fun and entertainment. The same at work places in their different work units throughout China.

We visited the kindergarten. It had four classrooms of mixed ages, three to five years. They performed for us, music and dancing, while we filmed them on video camera and took photographs.

We invited the teachers to come to the lecture room one afternoon to see the film. We were very surprised when toiling up six flights of stone stairs came the entire intake from the kindergarten. Settling their little legs into the seats, we began the show. The children's delight when they saw each other and their friends on the screen was touching. My own doctor students were also present, somewhat bewildered by their lesson being invaded by all these tiny children. After the film they all left quietly with their teachers – a great success all round.

## Wuhan sounds and smells

I remember the many sounds of Wuhan, from the early morning loudspeaker which exhorted us to get up, exercise and study, followed by strident music and the National Flag March. Every school and place of education has a daily flag ceremony. The red flag with five yellow stars is hoisted to the strains of the music while the students stand to attention and salute the flag as it is raised.

During the day constant shouting is to be heard, which is the normal speaking level between two or more people in China. It often appears as if they are having a row, but it is just the way they communicate.

Market sounds include lively banter between the stallholders. Ships, boats and sailing vessels hoot constantly along the river all day and night. Building work is non-stop. Outside our apartment a new building to house medical supplies was in progress. We had ear splitting decibels from early morning and all through the night for months. Sometimes, during a lull, would come the plaintive notes of a flute or Chinese pipes.

Television was often watched by the community outside in the street, one TV to fifty or more people crowding round to watch the latest Dynasty type soap, Han, Qing or Ming that is, not Joan Collins!

Sometimes a colourful procession would caper down the streets, with an old-style litter being carried by two men. Inside the carriage would be a lovely girl, like a bride dressed in the traditional costume. The leaders carried banners and performed a play all down the streets to amuse the peasants, it was in fact a political awareness campaign, but enjoyed by all.

There were two levels up the long market place. Little stone steps led upwards into a maze of tiny passages, where many older people lived. I saw women in dark blue trouser-suits with red armbands and was informed that they belonged to the street committee, it was their duty to report anything amiss amongst the neighbours. They kept a tally on who was moving in or out, who was expecting a baby, if they had one child already they were subjected to disapproval, and a heavy fine if they did not have it aborted. Families with more than one child were those who had given birth long before the new rule. This rule was imposed to try and curb China's huge population. In the countryside they were allowed to have more, as they are needed for work in the fields.

The street committee members were also there to give

any help or advice that they could, a neighbourhood watch type of set up. A small theatre was tucked away down a side street, nearly always closed. One day we saw big posters advertising a one day show of Chinese Opera. It was on all day non-stop. We crept in after paying a small amount, and were seated at the front in huge red velvet armchairs. The Opera was wonderful – great singing in their high pitched voices that defies description. The acrobatics were superb, the costumes immaculate and the story very funny. How this company found their way to the back street theatre in Wuchang I do not know, but for the one day the theatre was open in the two years we were there, it was worth the wait.

Chinese audiences are not the polite non-rustling audiences of the western world, half the fun is turning round to wave and shout to your friends, to eat, drink, spit and be merry. They rustle and rattle, move around, get up and down, block your view and to us are very antisocial.

Now mobile phones are added to the noise, oh yes, and non-stop flashing cameras. What a shock some Chinese visitors to the west must get on observing our theatre audiences.

Each place has its own unique smells. Wuchang had the dubious one of some very poor, public toilets. We called the area Pong Alley. Even the Chinese held their noses as they passed by. Luckily it was knocked down in our second year and new toilet facilities were available, with a woman and man waiting to take your coins. In return, customers were given a square of toilet paper, always pink and rough. There were basins with flush water taps. The toilets were always of the porcelain bowl, squat variety. Another street we named Tupperware Alley as it was given over to vendors selling all household goods, pots, pans, woks, clothes lines and pegs, wash bowls with enamel designs, mugs with lids, crockery and cutlery, scrubbing brushes and brooms, or just broom handles.

In spring a welcome sight were the flower sellers. They sold small, sweet-smelling jasmine blossom and magnolias. Later came sprays of yellow mimosa and red buds of plum blossom. Local gardens grew grapes, cucumbers, marrows and numerous fruits. Down by the Yangtze River, lively breezes brought a freshness to the air, tangy and crisp, away from the fumes and noise of traffic. The slap, slap of water against the sides of the bank, I never tired of watching the water traffic.

We sometimes travelled on the buses. The seats were wooden slats, if you were lucky enough to get one. It was always fun to observe the passengers. Adults everywhere are given seats as a priority, no standing up for adults. Heavy bags may include clucking hens. It is quite a feat to stand on some of these buses as their drivers are young and enjoy throwing their passengers around, it adds spice to their day.

The conductresses shout at passengers to come on their bus, laughing, good natured, always well dressed.

The sights, sounds and smells of Wuhan are not easy to forget.

# Chapter 9

## Shenzhen

It is not easy to settle down to life in your own country after some time abroad. You have taken on some of the culture and ideas of where you were living. Mass media and use of new words added to a language, influence you wherever you are in the world.

I would listen to people talking in England on our annual visits and found I did not understand them or the subject being discussed. The same with television and the soaps, new characters, and whole new families that I knew nothing about.

My ears had tuned into the Chinese language and ways of thinking. On Chinese television in Shenzhen, Guangdong province, we could get CCTV, (from Beijing) CNA an American station, and various local TV stations such as Nashan and Shenzhen.

In Wuhan we spoke on a local radio station (Chuntian) about our work in China. One of my students who lived on the college campus was a DJ for this radio company.

Whilst teaching and living in Shenzhen for six years, we both made several television appearances. One we did together was about married couples, we were the only foreign couple amongst a sea of Chinese.

I danced to my husband's playing the ukulele and singing 'On the Sunny Side of the Street'. Two others I did connected with education, talking about primary education and showing demonstration classes from the school at which I was working. We came to Shenzhen via invitation from our work in Wuhan. The large primary school in Shenzhen had just been built and we began at Shenzhen Nanshan Foreign Language School on its first opening day in 1995.

We were given basic accommodation and bicycles, as the school was some distance away. We attended the opening ceremony and raising of the flag. After meeting the Chinese English teaching staff we were given our timetables. These were changed three times within a week, so it was difficult to get organised. I was asked to teach Music, Art and Dance to ten different classes. I had a music room with a piano and used my own tape recorder.

Each class had forty-five to forty-seven pupils, they are called students in China from kindergarten upwards. Delightful children. They enjoyed learning English songs, drama and dances. We did lots of primary art work but I had to be very creative with materials as very little had been bought. I could find no paints, paper, or crayons – all basic materials.

Finally the pupils were asked to bring their own coloured pens etc and I bought typing paper from a nearby market, until stocks came into the school.

On our annual trip to the UK I supplemented the art and book supplies by buying and sending them to China via parcel post, a costly and laborious business. This was not reimbursed but made my classes much more fun and easier to deal with so many children at once. Teaching generally is its own reward, if you want money you don't go into teaching. Although that is not necessarily true of England today.

My classes were year one, two, three and five. This included the ages of six to eleven years. We also taught a Saturday morning class called Activity classes. I did English and Drama with the older pupils. All the classes were conducted in English.

The Chinese teachers teach only one subject. They do not have our system of a primary teacher teaching all subjects in one class.

The young pupils have a class teacher, who is in effect a Mother Hen, only there in between other teacher's classes, to prepare books for the next subject.

The class teaching is based on teaching from the text book every dot and comma, with seating in formal straight rows.

The first headmaster wanted to introduce a more flexible, creative approach, and this was where I was asked to develop the teacher's knowledge and understanding. The headmaster, Mr Lan, had written some basic English books with nice illustrations which had been published and acclaimed as revolutionary for China. He asked me to write some stories for future issues. I did eight books in collaboration with him and the Nanshan Education Bureau. I also had a children's book of my own published within the same series, in which I used my own illustrations.

One or two amusing cultural differences happened during the pre-publication. One of my illustrations showed a 'Yy' for yellow sun, in China the sun is called red, so this had to be changed. All the children drew red suns, never yellow.

My husband and I had to get used to shopping and cooking on calor gas again. We were already experienced, old hands from Wuhan but everywhere is different. Shenzhen is situated on the Pearl River Delta in South China. It is sub-tropical, very hot and humid most of the year and never goes below the sixties (f). Flowering trees, plants and fruits are abundant. Banana and lychee plantations are everywhere. Shenzhen used to be a sleepy, backwater, fishing village ten years or so ago. Today it is one of the most thriving special economic zones in China.

The buildings are spectacular and rival those of its

next door neighbour from across the water, Hong Kong, which is only an hour away by ferry or train.

Shenzhen is known as the Garden City. Its gardens, parks and several international, world-renowned golf courses are beautifully kept. The main roads have developed over the last five years, to improve heavy congestion on the busy roads. Delightful roads now run straight by the side of the Pearl River, all with lovely landscaped gardens on either side. Fishing nets can be seen on the mud flats, and the mountains rise all around the sandy bays.

The roads are too busy for safe cycling and there are few cycle paths. You can use scooters, cars, buses and taxis. We began by travelling around on local buses. These are driven by young men with a death wish for themselves and their passengers. We were fortunate in not being involved in an accident but there were many. These buses had conductors or conductresses whose job, apart from collecting money was to screech through an open window and try to attract as many passengers to travel on their bus as possible. They held up hand written placards to say where they were bound. Would-be passengers stopped them and argued the price before boarding, all very entertaining but annoying when you were in a hurry. Taxis were safer, reasonably priced especially when you spoke to them in Chinese, which was a necessity, some of them also being illiterate in their own language. The train to Hong Kong meant either a car or bus of an hour's journey to the station, followed by tedious form filling and long queues for customs. The train, when you finally did board, was comfortable, fast and efficient, the route pleasant and scenic, through towns and villages of the New Territories.

My favourite mode of travel to Hong Kong for our innumerable weekend jaunts from Shenzhen, was by ferry from Shekou. This route was only a twenty minute taxi ride from our school apartment.

We still had to fill in a form and go through the customs but it was quick and uncrowded.

Shekou is on the border between China's mainland and Hong Kong. It is closely guarded against people who try to slip in and out undetected. Border guards sit in high watch towers overlooking the river. The shoreline has been fenced off around the gardens of the local five-star hotel call the Nanhai.

We did most of our shopping at the local supermarket as they catered for foreign tastes. Foreigners come to Shekou to work for big companies, mainly oil industries. Americans, Scandinavians, Russians and Europeans. We rarely met foreigners in Nanshan. For our first four years at the school we were the only foreign teachers.

We also taught Business English at some big companies such as the Hwawei, the telecommunications, the Futian Industrial Bank and Shenzhen University.

The work possibilities for good English teachers today are limitless in China. Shenzhen is full of rich Chinese. They pay for their children to have extra coaching. Many Chinese teachers work at the weekends to supplement their low wages.

The Chinese teachers at our school came from all over China, Mongolia, Jilin in the North, Wuhan, Zinjiang, Xian, North, South, East and West. To become a citizen of Shenzhen is not easy, as workers can get up to three times the salary of other places in China, Shenzhen is naturally a Mecca. The authorities demand citizenship entries by examination. Only a few succeed.

# Chapter 10

## Economy and Crime

### Rising Wealth

As China has opened its policies to the outside world, huge leaps have taken place in socio-economic terms, with specially designated economic zones, especially around coastal areas. The industry in the Wuhan area is mainly iron and steel. In Shenzhen, Guangdong Province it is a mix of high finance, international banking, big companies with import and export, technology, telecommunications, computing, scientific programmes and science and industrial parks for research and global business.

Nanshan Foreign Language School is situated at the top of a hill on a Science and Industry Park. Many of the students' parents work in this park. They are the white-collar workers, with degrees and high expectations for themselves and their children. They live in homes bought up by their companies. They are usually of a medium to high standard, blocks of apartments which vary from two to three bedrooms, sitting room, kitchen and bathroom plus balcony and landscaped, private gardens. The grounds are manned twenty-four hours by gate officials, who check each person and car which comes in and out. Around the school are some pink and white tiled blocks of apartments. Inside they are modern, light and airy, five storeys high, with every modern convenience.

We have basic accommodation, small rooms and cheap but serviceable furniture. As the school canteen is on the ground floor, rats and cockroaches are unpleasant visitors around the messy bins. The Chinese teachers have the typical peasant habits of dropping food everywhere, thrown on to the floor and left open to the heat and flies. Luckily we live on the fifth floor. Mosquitoes are another thing to avoid. We have always had mosquito nets around our beds in China. We use electric mosquito coils and burning coils around the rooms. We do get bitten sometimes and then use special oils or cream quickly to avoid itching and swelling. It is essential to have injections against all the tropical diseases you can catch when living abroad.

Another trick is to wear protective clothing from dusk onwards, long sleeves, skirts or trousers and the use of an anti-repellent cream. Dusk is a pleasant time for a walk, after the heat of the day, this is when the toddlers appear with the grandparents for their airing.

Nearly all apartments have an iron barred security door in front of the usual wooden one. These are closed and the inner one left open for coolness. All family life is on full view at all times of the day, privacy is not valued as in the West. Some of these iron gates are works of art in the more expensive areas.

As Shenzhen has increased in wealth so has the crime rate risen. Petty thieving of bikes is a major crime.

We experienced two break-ins to our apartment, one before the security gate and bars at the windows and around the balcony were fitted. The first one was a thief who threw a rope with grappling hook over the balcony and quietly climbed up.

Luckily my husband, who could not sleep because of the heat, was sitting in the living room with no light on. He saw the large shadow of the thief trying to open our door from the balcony, he yelled. The thief dropped quickly to the ground and was away.

The next day it was discovered that two teachers had their bags stolen, they had slept with doors and windows open.

Security gates and bars were then fitted throughout the school.

Our second unwelcome visitor we believe came from the inside. My husband had received his monthly pay and had prepared it prior to going to the bank the next morning.

We had arranged an early car to deliver this money. The next morning I saw his briefcase had been moved from where he left it. We discovered the window lock had been forced and found footprints on the table below. Someone had been in our apartment as we slept and taken the briefcase which also included his passport. Again this was before we had bars over the window.

The Public Security service was brought in and the usual details taken. However by looking around the building and on the different floor levels, my husband found his own abandoned brief case and luckily with passport still intact, but alas no money.

He was very relieved to get his passport, it causes a lot of problems if you lose or have your passport stolen. The PSB call on all foreigners to give them a pep talk on how to behave in their country and to tell them the rules. It is efficient and fair. It can be rather alarming though to have them hammering on your door at bedtime demanding to see your papers without any warning. The school dealt with our paperwork but if anything was out of order, they could be heavily fined.

# Medicals and public viewing

Each year we had to undergo a medical whilst in China. This was paid for by the education bureau and involved a trip to a local hospital or clinic for checks on heart, blood pressure, lung and chest X-rays, pulse rate, weight and height measurements. We were moved around from one room to another, filled in numerous bits of paper and tried out our medical Chinese.

In six years I only had to visit the dentist one. All doctors and dentists work at the hospitals, there are no private surgeries except perhaps in Hong Kong. The treatment is always good and inexpensive, but the hygiene not what we are used to however. It is also open house for anyone to wander in and watch what is happening. I am not too keen on strangers walking up to me in the dentist's chair and peering into my mouth. It is the same in hospital – unless you close the door, which Chinese people do not, you have complete strangers wandering in to stare at you. Everyone must pay for their treatment and medicines in China. Help is available to those with the lowest incomes but the cost is generally kept low.

In the street I got used to people staring, being blonde and blue eyed, it always aroused curiosity. Quite a few babies would cry when they saw me, most disconcerting.

Real criminals such as armed robbers, murderers, rapists and drug runners get the death penalty. Public executions are still held in Shenzhen. The faces of those to be executed plus the place and date are exhibited in public places. These are usually young men, but sometimes women. Information is then given that the execution has taken place.

The bill for the bullet that kills them is sent to their parents. Disgrace follows the whole family – a strong deterrent one would imagine but as the economy grows so to does the crime rate. As Shenzhen is on the three borders with Thailand, Vietnam and Burma, many drugs now pass through. Lorries block the highways on their way to Europe and the West, giving more opportunities for smuggling. It is a huge gamble with life.

# Chapter 11

## Buildings and Neighbours

Shenzhen is surrounded by small mountains, which are continually being levelled by machinery for building materials and space. We have seen the views from our fifth floor apartment totally altered within six years.

An old burial ground on one hill had its big urns removed for building purposes. Tractors and lorries, big cranes and thumping earth-flatteners have also followed us wherever we have settled. The heat, humidity, noise and dust is indescribable.

Noisy neighbours also shout, bang and incessantly chop things, morning, noon and night. The chopper cuts all food into tiny swallow size morsels ready to throw into a hot oiled wok. Television, radio, tape recorders and karaoke reverberate around the concrete block after a day's teaching.

Below one window was like a refugee camp. Families of building contractors lived miles from their villages, in make-shift houses on the baked, red earth, thrown together from wooden packing cases, tin roofs and any other spare materials. These gypsy-style people had electricity (where from was a mystery), and two open wells for water. They shrieked and cuffed their offspring, washed and pounded their clothes by the open wells, made vegetable plots to hoe and water, and cooked on open fires.

A standpipe was used for bathing and cleaning teeth. Babies and children had their hair scrubbed hard under the cold water. They somehow kept themselves and their clothes clean amongst all the dust and debris.

Festivities were celebrated such as the Moon Festival, and Qing Ming (ancestor worship). As the moon rose fully, the families sat around their doorways with candles glowing inside jam jars on the upturned crates. A few cakes and some fruit were placed alongside joss sticks as offerings to their Buddhist beliefs.

The men, scrubbed and wearing clean white shirts, would meet their friends for a beer and a game of pool or cards. Pool was a popular pastime, always played outdoors in the market place. There were cheap dance halls and cinemas, even a roller-skating rink.

For other wealthier folk, downtown Shenzhen could off all the glitter of big cities, restaurants, discos and dance halls, nightclubs and bars. Young people from Hong Kong would come over, for the entertainment is cheaper on the mainland. Drugs are also easy to obtain. The police have regular crack-downs on dubious nightclubs, prostitution and gambling. Many wealthy businessmen resort to bigamy or keep two families, one in Shenzhen the other in Hong Kong, shades of the dynasty days of keeping concubines.

The modern Chinese girl of today knows what she wants too. A big house, servants, money, a car and a man with good prospects, love rarely comes into the equation. Television soaps are full of dramatic love triangles but it is really looking at the mercenary side of new modern China.

Foreigners are fair game for the marriage stakes. Any single man or woman can be taken in by the whiles of Chinese smooth-talkers, while all they want is a passport abroad, preferably to the USA.

It is fascinating watching a society changing, our own included. China has a lot to learn from the West, but equally we can learn a lot from Eastern philosophies.

# Chapter 12

## Primary Education

School life begins early in China. We rise at 6 a.m., have breakfast in our apartment and first lessons begin at 8 a.m. Each class lasts for forty-five minutes. I finished up with between twenty two and thirty classes a week. Most Chinese teachers have between five and twelve classes a week. I am paid per class, they are paid a set salary monthly, regardless of the number of classes they take. All the money is in renminbi (people's money).

The Chinese teaching is formal and by the book. Grammar is gone into in great detail. My way is more creative and involved getting the children to communicate in English, to think and do things for themselves, to cooperate with each other, to learn to use different mediums and learn rules via suitable games. To use English as a medium for oral, reading, listening, writing, Maths, Science and Arts and Crafts, dance, drama and PE, I emphasised the use of the five senses. We also have outdoor nature lessons and observations.

During my fourth year with the third headmaster, I was asked to design a large room in my own style, suitable for group teaching rather than the formal rows to which they were used. I drew up my plans, including the shapes of the tables. The room was prepared, decorated and furnished – what a contrast to the other classrooms, it was a delight to work here. We had space, light, pastel coloured, octagonal stacking tables and matching chairs, with concealed lighting in the ceiling, carpet at one end, blue and white floor covering on the rest of the floor, plus long book shelves. The overall colour was blue and white. The furniture was pink, lilac, pale green and blue. I was asked what I would like to call the room. It went from the original idea of the Blue Room to the Rainbow Room.

The children were awed initially but not for long, once they grasped that we sat on the carpet, found out their tasks for the lesson, then they were away. Forty-five pupils and one teacher!

It was a job to get round all of them and develop their language skills in their different tasks, but we managed and monitors were appointed for clearing up etc. Each part of the room was set out for different purposes. We had science tables, a listening corner, reading area, writing area, art and crafts tables and English and Maths games. They learned dominoes, matching cards and lotto, jigsaws, puzzles, naming animals, flowers and trees.

I made pastry for cooking. They made woolly balls, did colourful friezes, painting, sewing cards, Lego and project work, all the things familiar to an English primary teacher but revolutionary for Chinese teachers. I provided all the materials from books to games, old radios, magnets, art materials etc; I sent them from the UK during my holidays.

These pupils varied from between five and eight years and I gave them tasks according to their abilities.

I had to be slick in preparing the class between each session. I had no more than ten minutes in which to check everything was cleared and set out ready, before going to another building to collect the next class. These ten minutes were supposed to be a break but I never got one, it was a toss up between a visit to the toilet or grabbing some hot water for a drink.

It would have been much easier to have a helper but no one was available. The NUT (National Union of

Teachers) would not have put up with many things that I had to during this time.

Nanshan Foreign Language School is a Government-funded school. The parents have to pay for uniforms, outings, meals and transport.

I also taught at two kindergartens twice weekly. The policy in China today is for young children from as early as two years old to be exposed to an English learning environment. My two and three year olds learnt their colours and numbers, simple songs, different art activities and small projects such as things connected with water, where we had great fun with bubble blowing. Each child had a straw and blew big masses of bubbles then blew them up into the air. We looked at the different colours and sizes, later we did experiments with balloons. Other games involved social skills and safety training. Constructive games involved putting on their own shoes, coats etc, in teams. Young children have a short attention span so need stimulation, constant attention and different tasks. Quality in education is now stressed rather than quantity. This stresses the overall development of each pupil, not just exam marks or individual subjects. Questions have been raised in China about the amount of homework for school children and that the heavy burden should be lifted. Their school bags are certainly heavy as they carry all their books from one class to another. They study many different subjects daily.

Music is well taught, there is a choice of traditional Chinese instruments or international instruments. They can learn piano, violin, recorder, cello, flute and bassoon trumpet etc. The traditional instruments include the two stringed er-hu from the Sung dynasty. The dizi is a bamboo flute used as a solo instrument also in orchestras. The jing-hu used to accompany Chinese opera. Another bowed instrument, the pi-pa, has been used for over two thousand years. It has between nineteen to twenty-six bamboo frets glued on to the under part of the lute, which together with the six ledges are arranged as stops. There are three kinds of strings. These are made of steel wire covered with silver, or nylon, or silk strings. There are four strings on a pi-pa, a delicate-sounding plucked instrument. Others include the suo-na, an ancient wind instrument, sometimes called a la-ba, made of wood with a metal bell at one end and a straw double reed at the other. The yang chin is the Chinese dulcimer, played with two bamboo sticks. It is one of the principal instruments in a Chinese Orchestra.

Chinese dance training is strict, similar to Western ballet training. Fluid and graceful, young Chinese girls and boys can bend and kick high, their trained young acrobats on stage are world beaters. The art training is very formal, and does not allow for freedom of expression. The same with more academic subjects, a basic ground knowledge of science, history, physics, geography and maths seems to suffice. All exams are graded by teachers and are given very high grades in order to satisfy parents; they are not realistic. If they attend classes, sit, listen and read and write, they can attain 100% with no difficulty. The same applies right through the education system. This will gradually change as they have to compete with Western ideas and learn to develop and extend their own ideas, learn to be constructive, enquiring and questioning. However we have made a start at the early years level.

A typical day is not so easy to describe as all days bring a few new surprises, however, I can outline a teaching day via the timetable. The pupils are collected from their homes by school coaches, of which there are now eighteen. Some children are brought by car and local children walk with their parents or grandparents. The distances range from two to around ten miles. They all arrive for 7.30 a.m. They have breakfast in their classrooms. Silver trays with hollows of different sizes and shapes hold different foods – white rubber-type dough rolls or deep fried dough sticks, thin rice porridge call congee, hard boiled eggs, or cold meat and cake. They bring their own cups and boxed drinks and can get boiled water or cooled water from a machine in each classroom at any time of the day.

The first lessons begin at 8 a.m., usually taken by the class teacher. I like these early classes, the pupils are alert and receptive. There are four periods during the morning with very short breaks between. Lunch is also served in the classroom. The canteen staff bring many heavy canisters over from the kitchens on the back of tricycles. Each class has monitors, who take the canisters to their class and serve the hot meals to the waiting hordes! Usually rice or noodles, meat or fish and vegetables. The teachers have lunch in the canteen where the meals are free and given out in return for meal tickets which are issued in booklets. The dining room is where teachers catch up with the latest gossip or have a moan as teachers do, it is a good place for socialising.

We cooked and ate in our apartment, mainly because we liked our own style of cooking better. Also we appreciated the quiet, after a morning in school. Lunch times are staggered for the staff, and begin from eleven-thirty until twelve-thirty.

Then it is Xie Xie (rest time) for all, for the next two hours. As the weather is mostly hot and humid and the pupils and staff have been up and about since dawn, this rest is much needed.

I managed to cook, eat, rest and read or just sleep.

Classes started again at two-thirty. During the afternoon many classes are given over to sport, art, PE, dance and music. English classes and Chinese classes continue all through the day. The school day for primary school students finishes at 5 a.m. and the buses take them home. Middle school students stay on to do their homework in the early evening, before returning home at 7.30. They have the afternoon periods free for games or rest periods as they wish.

An international-size running track runs outside our building. In the grassy centre football is played. There are long jump sand pitches, parallel bars and plenty of gym equipment. The sports training is rigorous. Pupils run to the point of exhaustion in the humidity, which to me seems pointless. Red perspiring faces, hardly able to breathe with the exertions. Showers are available on every corridor for use afterwards.

Competition is strong in the Nanshan district. Every day some class is preparing for a competition. Sometimes it is for English oral work, or essay writing, drama, an art exhibition or musical performance.

I have been involved in several of these competitions both with the pupils and the teachers. My first was a drama contest in which the teachers had to write the drama that their students performed in front of judges, and a large audience at a chosen venue.

I wrote a simple story called 'The Hat', and it was performed by second and third year pupils. I designed the costumes and we had them made up – they were great!

Out of over a hundred entries our performance gained second prize. We received a long red velvet banner inscribed in gold characters with the names, event and date.

My second event was a teacher's aerobics contest. I was invited to join our teachers. The aim was to improve awareness of health and fitness for teachers in the area, it was hard work!

Our teacher, who was the PE expert, put us through our paces every day for six weeks. Press-ups and strong arm movements, we finally mastered our long routine. The contest took place in the dance studio of another local school. There were many school teams in jazzy coloured outfits. We were decked out in pink and black lycra leotards and shorts and white buckskin trainers, which we were allowed to keep.

Again we came second and received another big velvet banner and silver cup to swell the school trophies. I was the only foreigner involved, the judge called it 'An International Competition'. Joining in with the various activities is an important part of belonging and making friends in China. You are judged on what you do and how you approach things.

New teachers must prove their worth not by showing a degree certificate but via a demonstration class to everyone. They are hired or fired on the strength of their performance, experience and knowledge.

Chinese teachers get many opportunities to watch other teachers, both in their own school and in other schools. As an experimental school we have to give many demonstration classes for local schools, their Heads and staff and to overseas visitors.

Foreigners come for short periods to teach in Shenzhen, but rarely stay longer than a year. American University students have an exchange system, and our school in recent years has formed links with New Zealand, Australia, UK and Canada. Some exchanges are arranged during the long summer holidays.

The second longest holiday is the Spring Festival, which is in February/March, during which all teachers try to visit their families throughout China.

Teacher confidence is given a boost each new autumn semester. On the strength of their teaching performance throughout the previous year, a few teachers from schools throughout Guangdong Province are given special awards, red silk-bound books with certificates giving details of each award, place, name and date. Later a money prize is given out also to each award winner, some receive golden key pendants.

I have been lucky enough to receive five Advanced Teacher awards plus a drama certificate and a special one from the Science and Industry Business Community, and one from our own school called 'Advanced Scientific Teacher' signed by the third headmaster Mr Liu for the year 2000. These are a great honour as I do not know of any other foreigner being given these awards in Shenzhen.

Chinese ceremonies are long and full of speeches, usually followed by a concert of dance, singing and music. There is much shaking of hands, gifts and flowers presented and more speeches, it can go on for several hours. Patience is definitely a virtue in this society.

The use of English in China is often incorrect and rather flowery, but the meanings are generally understood. For example, in large letters over the front of Nanshan Foreign Language School are the words 'Knowing, Doing, Caring and Creating'.

The school policy includes 'STOB' Safety, Tidiness, Order and Beauty. The working standard is for 'High quality and efficiency'. The school slogan is 'Strive for perfection'. All worthy ideals. Around the school are many wall plaques with the sayings interpreted from Chinese characters to English, of famous men and women, from Deng Xiao Ping who says 'Education should meet the needs of modernisation, the world and the future', to Karl Marx, 'There is no royal road to science, and only those who do not dread the fatiguing climb of its steep paths have a chance of gaining its luminous summits'. Then Chekhov, 'Science is the most important thing that man ever requires'. Or William Shakespeare, 'Do not for one repulse, forego the purpose that you resolved to effect'.

Other plaques have quotations from famous world philosophers.

In between these illustrious sayings are small plaques in blue and white lettering to remind everyone on how to behave around the campus. One has the message, 'Keep your hands to yourself'. Others 'Do not litter', 'Use water carefully', and around the gardens, 'Pick me up to keep beautiful' (meaning litter), and so on. The literal interpretations from one language to another cause some problems and for us a daily smile.

I was asked to write out suitable notices for around the campus, which I did, but along the way they got interpreted into Chinese English, or as we call it 'Chinglish'. However, I keep reminding myself that I would have the same problems if I had to write them in Chinese characters. Any correct interpretations asked for by Chinese English teachers are listened to but never done as you have advised. The same with any written material.

I took both day and evening classes in English for the staff and visiting staff from other schools around Nanshan District. Sometimes they asked for lectures on specific subjects, others were interactive classes and also some sessions included Information Technology classes in order to understand computer English. All the pupils learn computing throughout the school. There are nearly 2000 students and 186 staff of which 121 are teachers. Most of them are graduates, some are technical training graduates. From the year 2000, all teachers had to attend English classes in the evening, these were divided into three groups, beginners, intermediate and advanced.

I took the advanced classes which included the heads of each department and the headmaster. Sometimes visitors would attend from the Nanshan Education Bureau. The other classes were taken by Chinese English teachers. I enjoyed these sessions. I later found out that they were more interested in my teaching methodology than the English. I admired the Headmaster for taking part in front of his staff, he also took the exam at the end of the term. This had been a requirement known to all but me. I was informed the night before that we would have an exam the next day.

Teaching in China could be frustrating, but never dull! The summer term 2000 was perhaps the most rewarding of the six years as I was able to teach in a much more creative way, which was better for the students.

The physical arrangements in the Rainbow Room gave access to areas of learning that had not been possible in the formal set-up. One morning I arrived early, as I usually did, in order to check everything before the classes began. A breathless young teacher rushed up to me and said that the Nanshan television would be coming to televise my classes. No prior warning, the typical Chinese way. They came and made a good recording, which was shown on the Nanshan news a few days later, and also on 'Pearl News' which is shown in Hong Kong. This was mostly in Chinese and English when I was asked for my educational views.

After this, came the television crew from Shenzhen TV. They made another programme which took a lot of time and effort on my part as they wanted a specific theme of their choosing, I did all that was requested including a huge finger-painted dragon by the children on a large piece of white cotton. This time the pupils were interviewed and the whole programme, apart from the actual English language used during the class, was in Chinese. The interesting part was that when the interviewer asked the pupils questions in Chinese, they answered in excellent English and they were only six and seven years old.

I was promised a video tape from each company. I received one from Nanshan TV, but nothing from the

Shenzhen company. The school got a lot of free publicity, which resulted in an influx of visitors from as far away as Australia, New Zealand, Canada, Japan, Hong Kong, Beijing, and more local parts of Guangdong. Our classes were watched, recorded on video cameras, and the pupils and classroom and its activities photographed in detail.

A third large building on the Science and Industry campus was secured for use as a kindergarten for the NFL school.

This was set up and the classrooms arranged as near as they could manage to imitate the Rainbow Room. The same furniture, similar equipment and so on BUT the teachers still arranged the furniture in rows and taught in the traditional style. One teacher, one subject. It takes time to train people to try new ideas.

The parents were in favour of new style teaching and I received some very nice emails from parents who had seen the TV programmes.

There is much work to be done in education in China but they are making rapid progress. A combination of the best of both systems would seem to be a sensible path to follow. The internal management varies from head to head, but all three at this school have had good influences on the progression of the new modern China's educational reforms. Many teachers are being encouraged to travel and work in schools, universities and colleges in other countries. Several have been abroad whilst we have been working in Shenzhen and they have returned to pass on what they have learnt.

# Chapter 13

## A Special Mountain

One of my favourite half-term holidays was one arranged by the Hubei Education Authorities for its foreign teachers.

A coach arrived to pick us all up from our different work units around the Wuhan area. We were bound for the Wulingyuan Mountains in Hunan Province. It was a long but scenic journey past farms, paddy fields and small country villages. At one point we had to cross a river on a ferry. We stayed overnight at a cheap Chinese hostel in dormitories. The next day we finally arrived at our destination, a newly-acclaimed nature reserve. The Wulingyuan mountain scenery is breathtaking. After the coach went as high as possible, we got out thankfully, and began to climb and explore.

There are towering rocks of many strange shapes, wide streams and creeks. Ninety percent of the area is covered by forest, here are rare wild flowers and medicinal herbs, birds and animals.

We followed a path upwards and I counted three thousand rough-hewn steps on the way up to the inevitable temple at the top, with wind chimes swinging in the clear mountain air. We saw a young Chinese couple in ethnic dress, he was playing a wooden flute while she danced amongst the trees.

We walked through tall thickets of bamboo, saw huge sprays of wild roses cascading down the ravines, and the forest was lit by a blaze of rhododendrons and azaleas. An unforgettable experience, especially the aching leg muscles after descending the steep, three thousand steps to the bottom.

You need stamina to see the lovely places China has to offer. On the same climb, I saw masses of wild blue iris, marshland orchids and a flower I could not identify, it was white and glowed with a halo effect coming from its centre.

Many flowers, such as the rose and rhododendron that we think of as English flowers, had their origins along with many others in China. Their seeds were gathered by plant hunters and brought back to Kew Gardens in London during the early nineteenth century.

It was so peaceful deep in the mountain forests, with clear waters running down the sides of the steep slopes, waterfalls in the deepest parts. Huge multi-coloured butterflies and dragonflies fluttered and hovered between the dappled plants.

Near the top was a pleasant place to eat, a long hut with wooden furniture, we were glad to sit with a drink and snack. We had been walking all morning for several hours. A little higher up, we came to a village square where the locals were well prepared with the usual trinket trays and drink vendors. The sun was hot, once outside the shelter of the bamboo tree and vines, we all flopped down on the grass. That night we slept in a small hostel half way down the mountain, it was in an idyllic place, but run down and damp. The electricity went out for the night, which meant going to bed early, which I for one did not mind. The next day the coach made its way back to our original hostel with dormitories. I much preferred the mountain hostel, despite no lights.

As this was a short trip, we were on our way the next day and travelled for many hours to reach Wuhan.

We enjoyed many short trips during our years in China. Sometimes they were just day outings, others for a long weekend, and some during the summer holidays. In Shenzhen we visited Honey Lake, Evergreen Nature Resort, the zoo, and numerous big parks, some with a fairground.

# Chapter 14

## Overseas Chinese & Tourist Attractions

One year we set off during the Spring Festival with the other Chinese teachers, we were to travel to Malaysia, Singapore and Thailand. It was the first time abroad for most of the teachers. There was a guide but it took a frustratingly long time to get through customs and to board the plane. The same in Malaysia, the guide talked non stop in Chinese only, for hours on the coach. The meals we stopped for were poor quality and we were shunted around, without any break from setting off at 4 a.m. that day until 10 p.m. We finished up again at the top of a steep mountain called the 'Highlands'. We had to go by chair lift over the rain forests to the Casino-styled hotel at the top.

My husband became ill and we decided to leave the fast-paced group and have a holiday on our own. We lost our fare and return flight but couldn't face any more tight organisation and non-stop moving. What we did find was the most wonderful hotel I have ever seen, the Palace of the Golden Horses in Kuala Lumpur. Here we stayed and recuperated until it was time to return to Shenzhen.

The Chinese mostly travel in organised groups and have little idea about how to make travel arrangements. They move together and miss so much through lack of initiative but that is the way they have accepted. They do have constant company to enjoy, but many on that trip came back exhausted.

It was our last venture at a long holiday with a unit.

Another year we went to Bali during the Spring

Festival. We usually went back to the UK but decided to have a change. We left a very cold winter behind and flew into glorious sunshine. We spent the whole holiday swimming, relaxing, watching the famous Balinese dancers and eating the excellent Indonesian cuisine. We visited one or two famous art centres with batik printings, wood carvings, oil paintings and pottery, the local volcanic mountain and an Indonesian Museum.

The Balinese are charming and laid back. They wander around with fresh white and gold Frangipani flowers in their hair (both men and women) and wear tie-printed sarongs. Every day you could see people carrying fruit and flower baskets to their gods, they would walk sometimes down to the sea and float their offerings on the blue-green waves.

The gentle manner vanished when a sales person approached, they would fling open a tray full of watches or silver jewellery and demand you look and buy. They were so pushy in their insistence that they spoiled an idyllic holiday for many people. The same on the beach, vendors waking you up to sell hats or bikinis. Other visitors had their hair plaited into many tiny plaits for an expensive hair-do done on the spot in the street, I did not partake.

Bali is a beautiful island but we could feel underlying tensions in the air everywhere we went.

Of all the places we visited for a holiday, I preferred Hainan Island in Southern China.

The most beautiful places in China for me were Hangzhou East Lake, Guilin and the Yangtze River.

# Hong Kong

Hong Kong was under British rule for many of the years we were in China. We were present at the hand-over in 1997 back to China. The mainland had been preparing for this big event for many months. The schools were arranging big concerts, the PLA (soldiers) and other military forces were preparing with meticulous precision for the march pasts on the great day of the return of Hong Kong to the motherland.

A week's holiday was declared from Beijing for all educational institutes and other places of work. My husband and I arranged to stay on Hong Kong Island, near the site where the handover was to take place.

A huge platform and tiered seats were erected for the actual hand-over ceremony in the square. The days leading up to the great day were counted by the minute on huge clocks all over the island, on television, everywhere there was a fever of anticipation. Music was specially composed; art work competitions abounded, including flag designs to show a new emblem for Hong Kong. The one finally used shows the national flower, the bauhinia, red on a white background. Special commemorative stamps were issued and many souvenirs were sold to cover the event of the century.

It was a happiness tinged by sadness for some. It had been Deng Xiaoping's greatest wish to live long enough to witness this historic occasion. Sadly he died on February 21st 1997 at the great age of ninety-two, just a few months before the hand-over. How proud he would have been of the immaculate performances given out on television of the parade of the PLA (Peoples Liberation Army), its air force, navy and vehicles. Deng had long acted as the final authority on Hong Kong policy, he had always had the final say in any friction concerning the territory. Stability became especially important with the arrival of the Special Administrative Region (SAR). This was to help the world to understand the concept and smooth-running of the one country, two systems, and to show its successful running.

At that time the vice premier and foreign minister was Qian Qichen, the most senior official in charge of Hong Kong affairs. Lu Ping, Director of the HK and Macau affairs office was the top man on routine policy affairs. These two leaders dealt directly with the still-present (at time of writing), Chief Executive Designate, Tung Chee-Hwa. Final matters on major policies however are to be controlled by the Politburo.

So from the joint agreement in 1984 which Margaret Thatcher signed, supported and watched by Lady Evans and Sir Richard Evans, the British ambassador, Lady Howe and Sir Geoffrey Howe, and Sir Percy Craddock for the British side, and Deng Xiaping, Liannian, Ji Pengfei, Wu Xueqian, Yao Guang and Xu Jiatun for the Chinese, to the present day hand-over ceremony.

This was a time of personal sadness for the then British Governor Chris Pattern, his wife, Lavinia and their daughters. Whether he had been popular in his post or not, he had enjoyed a most interesting and enviable life style. He was obviously very sad to leave. Prince Charles was at the closing ceremony and deserved all credit for sitting through the long speeches in torrential pouring rain.

At the newly-built Cultural Centre the royal yacht was moored. At the climax of this well-covered event was a spectacular firework display, as Hong Kong and, on the other side of the Pearl River, the mainland shouted with joy at their reunification. Prince Charles and Chris Pattern and family were slowly leaving Victoria Harbour with tears in their eyes. Another era had ended for the British.

Chris Pattern predictably settled down to writing a book of his years experiences as Governor to Hong Kong.

He has returned several times as a guest and been warmly welcomed. The thing I remember most is that he enjoyed a special custard pie made locally and had them sent up to the imposing white Government House. It is such little things that help you remember the man behind the façade of fame.

We were caught in the middle, being British and yet having lived and worked in China for so long. We existed in a cultural no-man's land, well I did. It was great to have participated at this great event.

Likewise in future years we visited Macao, just after the second successful return of the small island to the motherland. Whatever the political concerns, we are caught up in the school preparations for these major events. The Chinese put on a wonderful show when it is required.

## Island Hopping

We took advantage of Hong Kong to visit some of its smaller islands. These included Macau, Lamma, Lantau and Cheong Chau.

Our first visit was to Lantau, the largest island which boasts the biggest outdoor Buddha in the world. We took a colourful junk to cross the water, we were the colourful ones at the end of this very choppy sea trip. The junk ploughed through the rough waves in a far from smooth ride. At Silver Mine Bay, we disembarked and thought there was no way we could return by boat.

However we now took a smooth local bus ride and sat back to enjoy the sights. We passed a large prison, then followed the winding road to a delightful coastal village, where we stayed to walk around. The houses were built on stilts at the water's edge, fishermen sat mending nets while the women did the shopping, chopping, cooking and attending infants. We crossed a river on a ferry which was 'manned' by two women who pulled on the two stout ropes to pull us across. This old system has now been replaced by a machine pulley. The sun was hot, everywhere people wore wide-brimmed hats, sometimes with black cloth hanging all around the edges to give even more protection. We continued on to the Po Lin Monastery for a vegetarian lunch shared with the monks in their dining room.

The huge bronze Buddha stood outside, with many steps leading up to its summit on route to the monastery and its pretty gardens. Unfortunately the Buddha was surrounded by bamboo scaffolding on the day we arrived for some restoration work.

We did return by boat and this time we had a smoother journey.

Today Lantau Island is known for its famous bridge linking Hong Kong directly by car and coach, and the direct trains straight through to the great new HK international airport of Chek Lap Kok.

Although further away for us than the old airport, it is much more convenient in so far as speed of arrival and efficiency, also luggage can be weighed in at the rail station. This new international airport is architecturally a triumph. The staff are friendly and efficient, the restaurants and shops of a high standard.

The old airport at Kai Tak retains its nostalgia for many who travelled frequently to Hong Kong. No one who travelled in those days will forget the landing. With your heart in your mouth you watched as the plane came down between high mountains onto a narrow runway built out to sea and just skimming the tops of high-rise blocks. More than once did some hapless pilot land in the water. The new airport affords a much higher degree of safety overall.

On arrival at HK after you have gone through the customs, you catch an airport train direct into Kowloon, with intermediate stops en route, or you can take a bus to various destinations. As the airport is so vast there is no feeling of a dense crowd and you are left with plenty of time to achieve all that is necessary.

Our favourite stop-over place was the YMCA at Victoria Harbour in Kowloon. We had a wonderful view over the harbour, directly opposite the Cultural Centre where hundreds of newly-weds pose daily. White weddings with beautiful dresses and lavishly decorated cars, they smile for hours in rain or shine, with many proud family members assisting. At the back of the Cultural Centre directly facing the sea wall and harbour and overlooking Hong Kong Island, are long shallow steps. Here the brides and grooms also pose for photographers.

Along the busy harbour you can watch the water traffic for hours, a never-ending colourful mix of boats from huge tourist ships bound for Vietnam, Hainan Island and the Mainland China coast, to little tugs pulling large coal barges; sleek fast speedboats of the police to fishermen's junks and a few sail boats. There is a constant criss-crossing of the famous 'Star Ferries' with their poetic names such as 'Morning Star', 'Starlight', etc.

I love to travel on the short distances between the two islands. The journey is cheap and full of interesting people. The views are spectacular, for me the journey is too short. You can, however, book for longer rides elsewhere. I travel on the Star Ferries for the exhilarating sea breezes and pleasure of being on the water.

We enjoyed many trips to Hong Kong both under British Rule and now Chinese Rule. People ask about the differences since the hand over. Many British and European people did leave the island before the hand-over. Initially there were fewer visitors, but today there does not outwardly appear much difference in day-to-day living.

Education however is going through major changes.

Hong Kong has long argued about the best language in which to teach its citizens. Cantonese is spoken by the majority of HK, Chinese, but they learn Putonghua and English. Some schools have taught in English only, others in Chinese only, some have tried classes using a mix of English/Cantonese/Putonghua. The result has been some very mixed-up teachers and students with low passes in some subjects. The level of spoken English is poor compared with the mainland, which is strange considering the years of British rule in HK. It is now imperative that the school children learn to communicate in Putongua, the Chinese of the mainland. Given a good tri-lingual background, these students can rely on good job prospects in the future. Kindergarten places are taken immediately, and the age for beginning English gets younger, at present they begin from two years. All this education comes at a high price in both the mainland and Hong Kong. Although schools may be run and partially paid for by the Chinese Government, the parents must contribute for many things. Private expensive education is more usual in Hong Kong. As housing and living expenses are also high, more and more families are buying property on the mainland. The nearest place with excellent housing for those who can afford it, is in Shenzhen. Here Hong Kong residents can buy property at a fraction of the local cost. Renting is also reasonable and cheap for those on a HK salary. An average two or three bedroom apartment in year 2001 cost around UK £200, rental per month, more for upmarket accommodation.

There are some excellent housing complexes, with lovely landscaped gardens and so much more space than Hong Kong. In the future it has been estimated that several thousand families will have moved to the quieter, less frenetic mainland.

Kowloon is known as one of the best shopping hubs in the world. It is packed with humanity, coloured neon lights, banners, goldsmiths, gadgets, computers and all the latest software and audio CD's, camera, copy watch merchants, tailors vie for your custom. Hong Kong is a vibrant, hard-selling city. It promises untold delights for unwary young men, with its wealth of nightclubs and Susi Wong's all waiting to pounce on their cash, credit cards and if possible passports to greater things.

The hotels and restaurants are mostly excellent, the quality of service and food unrivalled at the top hotels.

Hong Kong has something for everyone and we were thankful to be able to step out of our busy, demanding lives in Shenzhen for a feast of gourmet food and a soft bed occasionally.

Like London and other UK cities, HK has absorbed many different immigrants over the years, predominantly Indian and Philippines.

The splendid white mosque in Nathan Road is always busy with its Indian and other Moslem population. There are many churches of different Christian denominations including Catholic, Baptists, Latter Day Adventists, and so on. On Sundays the Victoria Harbour promenade seems to be taken over by masses of chattering, chanting, singing, bible-reading Philippinoes.

At other times they gather on their half days and spread around, sitting in groups on floor coverings, with picnic food, transistor radios, laughing and sounding like the twittering of a thousand sparrows. They are mostly young and flirt and dance, providing passers-by with free entertainment. These girls work in wealthy homes as maids, some are not treated well and reports are covered in the newspapers about the ill treatment some of them receive from their employers, but on these days of freedom they all seem happy.

The Indian community have existed for many years as restaurant owners; a few try their luck on the front trying to tell fortunes; others run successful tailors and sell Indian saris and silks. The infamous 'Chungking Mansions', a cheap haunt for many back packers, is full of good cheap eating houses and has many interesting market stalls on the ground floor.

Most tourists want to experience a ride on the Peak Tram Funicular that runs up to the top of the Victoria Peak. This tramway was built in 1885, it is so steep that you are lying back on the ascent, it is a great experience. There are several stations along the way. Built up the sides of the Peak are houses. The higher you go the more you move into the luxury belt. Here are the houses of the rich or belonging to companies to be let out to their employees. At the top you can obtain a wonderful all-encompassing view of Hong Kong and the harbour. Inside a large building are shops and restaurants, outside is a fountain which spurts different size jets of water in sequence, a cool place to sit and watch the passers-by. There are some lovely tree-shaded nature walks nearby.

Years ago I taught some pupils in Cumbria, who came from a home on the Peak. Hong Kong is not an easy place to live but it draws you back like a magnet.

## A Few Islands

Lamma is one of my favourite small islands belonging to Hong Kong. It is lush in tropical foliage and the delightful busy village at the bottom of the hill is full of interesting twists and turns. There is no traffic, just three-wheel vehicles for carrying luggage to the island's one hotel on the far side and for transportation of building materials and parcels from the ferry.

We hired bicycles to explore the area. Many open-air restaurants abound, from Chinese to Thai and Indian cooking. We enjoyed visits to the 'Bookworm Café', here you could enjoy healthy vegetarian meals or snacks, surf the net on computers and learn about local community events, it is also a second hand book store and is open seven days a week. This café is at the end of Yng Shue Wan Main Street. Continuing from there we found two small interesting Buddhist temples.

The road for the quayside rises quite steeply, we found our cycle hire shop halfway up the hill. Continuing upwards we passed huge banana trees full of fruit, and rosy pomegranates. Our first visit was quiet and peaceful, we passed pleasant houses and a school.

Riding along the country tracks without noisy traffic was a pleasure in itself. Eventually we found a charming bay in which to walk on the sand and paddle in the sea.

I could see a pagoda high on another hilltop and set off to explore. The cliff top was narrow so I left the bike and continued by foot. The views were great. The air smelt of warm fragrant flowers and aromatic plants. Many butterflies were enjoying the hot sun. The old island people wore protective headgear, usually the Guangdong style of straw hat, sometimes the women wore the Hong Kong hat with the black cloth around the brim. Small shops were full of beachwear, sweets, ice-cream and food.

Down near the harbour you could buy many types of fresh sea food.

At the top of the bay lay the island's one hotel, the 'Concerto Inn'. We spent a few days there but it was during the cold season. We still ate our meals outside, muffled up in all our clothes.

When I returned on a solo visit the following year the Inn appeared to be closed, but the Bookworm Café was still welcoming.

There are many good walks around the cliffs and across the island. The one thing that spoils its appearance is the large power station on one side near the sea. The advantages for the people who live there no doubt outweigh the disadvantages.

Several foreigners have made their base on Lamma Island whilst crossing daily to work on the ferry to Hong Kong, a short half-hour journey.

The living is cheaper and the atmosphere much more relaxed. For young children the island is a lovely place to live, for teenagers I imagine it would be too quiet.

## Cheung Chao Island

This island is a popular place for young Hong Kong couples and groups who want to spread their wings without adult supervision at the weekends.

As you step off the ferry, all along the front you see women sitting at tables with big books showing photographs of rooms to let.

You choose your room, pay your money and are given a key and instructions on how to reach your apartment.

We visited our first time with a young family we knew. Our apartment had a living room, two bedrooms and bathroom, an electric kettle to make tea and a table and chairs. Meals were bought in or eaten out. The block overlooked the beach and sea, which was very close. We slept at night to the sound of waves, very soothing. The island is small, and like Lamma has no traffic, except for a delightful toy-town type of fire engine.

Another pleasant place to explore and walk. You can go high up the mountainside. There are temples and a monastery, also a retreat for those inclined. We passed a very well kept cemetery garden. Each grave had a photo of the deceased and family details. Under the shade of indigenous trees, it was a tranquil place for a final rest.

In the village centre lies the Pak Tai Taoist Temple, which dates back to 1783 and was renovated in 1903. The Temple was dedicated to the god Pi Tai. A sword was found in the sea nearby dating back to the Sung Period (920-1279).

There is one big hotel but we were not impressed, it did not seem to fit the rest of the island in any way.

The ferries are frequent to and from both islands, Cheung Chao and Lamma.

The most interesting time to visit Cheung Chao is during the annual event call the 'Bun Festival'. This is a community effort and draws thousands of visitors each year. Towers of real buns, hundreds of metres high, are erected on bamboo scaffolding and placed in a prominent position. Many years ago a popular poet fell out with the Emperor over the taxes. Rather than pay the higher money demanded, the poet threw himself into the sea. The people came out and threw bread buns onto the water to stop the fish eating his body. Every year since, the poet has been remembered through the bun festival.

There is a long procession made up from different martial arts clubs and some local children are dressed to represent political figures or some famous person. They are then strapped to a bamboo frame and carried on the shoulders of young men, who are wheeled on cars. There are exciting displays of Kung Fu, Tai Chi, Qi Gong and dragon and lion dancers, drummers and musicians even Scottish pipers in full kilted splendour.

Taoist Monks join the parade to light joss sticks and pray at the Temples. The air is full of incense all around. The summer of 2001 was a very hot day for the Bun Festival and was enjoyed by several thousand spectators. Extra ferries ploughed back and forth day and night between Hong Kong and Cheung Chau.

It was a day to remember.

## Visit to Macau

I had always wanted to visit Macau, the Portuguese-owned territory off Hong Kong. The two and a half mile (four km) long by one mile (1.7 km wide) peninsula is situated at the mouth of the Pearl River. Regular ferries ran from Shenzhen or Hong Kong daily and the Macau/Chinese features were easy to spot amongst the vast crowds at the ferry terminus – dark, often wavy or curly hair and more Portuguese/Spanish faces and postures.

Before the hand-over of Macau to the motherland, the constant reporting of the Triads killing and maiming people on this small island put us off a visit. After the hand-over had been successfully made in year 2000, many of the Triad groups had been broken up by the PLA and gone to other pastures such as Shenzhen. We decided to go from Hong Kong.

We crossed on a hydrofoil and set off to explore, armed with a street map. From the modern arrival lounge, we stepped out into bright sunshine and found our way to a local bus stop to take us to the nearest central point of the town.

The first thing I saw from the bus window was names on the shop fronts in both Portuguese letters and Chinese characters. Having spent some time in Spain, it was like a homecoming to be able to read everything around us. The big, central square was full of lovely, pastel-coloured architecture, from the imposing Post Office to numerous small, delightful churches, pretty on the outside, cool and imposing on the inside.

The most famous landmark and place to be photographed are the ruins of St Paul's or Sao Paulo. This imposing façade is all that remains of one of the finest Christian buildings in the Far East. You approach it via a long, narrow, cobbled street bursting with vendors, little shops and colourful vitality, all uphill. The façade itself is reached after climbing many long, narrow, granite, stone steps. The first church was destroyed by fire in 1601, so Chinese and Japanese workers rebuilt a new church the following year. The Jesuits added a college but were expelled in 1762. In 1835 it was all destroyed, again by fire. In 1904 attempts to rebuild it were made but since then nothing has happened, except for the grand façade to become a famous monument visited by millions of tourists.

There are many interesting museums and historic buildings to visit, from the government house in pink and white, to the yellow and white Lisboa hotel, a mecca for gamblers. Many visitors come to Macau solely for the gambling; most Chinese love to gamble although it is supposed to be illegal.

There are several temples dating back to the Ming Dynasty around 1573 and a monument to Vasco da Gama, the great Portuguese discoverer and navigator, who set out from the Cape of Good Hope in 1497 and discovered the sea route to India.

You can visit the Dr Sun Yat-Sen Memorial House on the Avenida Sidonio Pais. This house contains documents on his life and photographs of Chiang Kai-Shek, founder of Taiwan. Sun Yat-sen was the leader of the Kuomingtang, a democratic, nationalist party. He is honoured as a liberator by the People's Republic of China and by the Taiwan government.

There are some excellent restaurants, the best to my mind offering the traditional Portuguese dishes. For our first meal we chose the typical peasants' fish soup. This is a big platter, including many shellfish and pieces of white fish in a garlic and saffron flavoured soup. Delicious with a glass of Portuguese white wine.

## Small Strands of Life

'When in Rome, (or in this case China), do as they do'. Well, this is certainly useful when it comes to having name cards printed. Everywhere you go there are new people being introduced, many issue invitations to further career prospects or the odd useful job. It is necessary to go through the ritual formality of presenting your name card, giving address, phone, fax and email address plus your qualifications and field of work. These cards must be given in two hands. They are received in the same manner, each giving a slight bow.

When discussing business, it is expected that you have asked about their family, health and continue small talk until they are relaxed. Next should come a meal and drinks. Discussions are still kept light and each side is weighing up the other, the social adaptability of a guest is a Chinese way of assessing foreigners. Dancing and singing after a meal are high on the agenda. The more important the guest the more lavish the banquet, always taken in a side room, not in a main busy restaurant with everyone else. Each restaurant has many smaller rooms for private parties.

After the meal, an outline of the proposed business

can be broached, followed up by a further meeting which this time will be business only.

I have watched with dismay the tactics of some business men, mostly Americans, who are used to a fast approach, and who bulldoze their hosts with business matters long before the Chinese have intended to make a decision. This only succeeds in putting them off and probably losing the business deal before it can get off the ground.

Patience, understanding of the culture, knowing the facial and body language and some Chinese language, are far better weapons in the world of finance and business deals. Your face either fits or it does not. The Chinese appreciate a quiet, honest approach but can also be hard-headed in the actual closing of any deals.

Any legal forms need to have interpreters to check on both sides of any deal. The Chinese, both male and female, are canny business partners.

Selecting your business card is another task. First find your shop, select from a book the type of print and picture desired, then select from different price ranges. We have always had cards ready whenever we go out. From Beijing to Wuhan to Shenzhen over fourteen years, I must have given out hundreds of cards and received the same back. Unfortunately the Chinese cards are often difficult to read to a Western eye. The best have them written as we do in both Chinese and English. We also gave our Chinese and English addresses.

Our personal mail was collected from the main gate of the College or school in pigeon holes. Sometimes the stamps had annoyingly been pinched off, by the Middle School students.

Luckily parcels and bigger packages had to be collected from the local Nanshan post office. This was a bus ride away but safer than being delivered to the school.

A chit of paper would be issued to the gatekeeper, who gave it to us for collection. Your passport details had to be recorded by the post office staff before your received your parcel. Likewise in Wuhan, although in those days you also had to pay several 'yuan' (monetary value), before they would release your goods.

How we welcomed parcels from England, especially around Christmas.

Easter and Christmas can be difficult times for expats. Special family times make you realise how foreign you are!

Our family were wonderful at writing letters and sending seasonal parcels and birthday gifts. I loved to receive books. The only place to get good up-to-date reading material was from Hong Kong, but they were so expensive. The best newspaper is the 'South China Morning Post' from Hong Kong but we could not get it delivered and read it when we frequented our favourite restaurant called Casablanca in Shekou. This restaurant is co-owned by a Swiss man and a Spanish man. The food was top class Western French and Italian style cooking. Here we could catch up with the world and local news. The papers were brought over on the ferry from Hong Kong at the weekends only.

I wrote some articles for the 'Shenzhen Daily'. This paper was written in Chinese characters but had an educational page in English every Monday. I collected my fees from the post office in the same manner as collecting a parcel, only this time I received the actual cash from the counter hand, carefully noted and stamped on several pieces of paper. Chinese bureaucracy is obsessed with form filling, which leads to endless problems if you lose these flimsy bits of paper.

I am often asked by people in the UK what I like about China? My answer is the people. They are quite innocent in so many ways, yet can be calculating when it comes to romance or marriage. They are a never-ending source of fascination, they pull together in adversity and knock down those who rise too quickly.

The older people are full of ways of making ends meet, they have learnt the hard way. It is a source of wonder to the old grandparents to go with their offspring and families to a McDonald's, their beaming faces accepting the better changes of economy all around them. They love to see their grandchild getting a good education and their own children living in their own apartment, still in many cases wearing the old, blue, high-collared suits for the men or floral trouser suits for the women, with their knife and fork hair cuts proclaiming them as part of the old China.

The young mothers posture in skimpy, tightly-fitting dresses or smart suits. They sport permed hair sometimes with blonde highlights which are actually dark red. The children are dressed in frilly party dresses or casual USA style of clothing. The Jones' concept of the Nouveau Riche is alive and well in Shenzhen and other affluent coastal areas of china.

Another thing said to me in the UK was 'Why go all that way to teach, why not help children over here?' My answer is that I have taught in England in the tough inner city London areas for over twenty years. I see no reason not to combine my love of travel with working for the UNDP (VSO) or for any other government in any part of the world. Children are children the world over. In London, they are from many countries and I have learnt to respect their culture, customs and language, whatever their origin.

Although I have taught many adults, children have always been my priority. China knows little about the West, they are just beginning to travel more freely. The more countries learn about each other and overcome fears caused by lack of knowledge, the better our chances for future world peace. It all begins at home and through education.

Not far from Nanshan is a place known as the Overseas Chinese Town. Here are good, well-built apartments, facilities, restaurants and shops. There are playgrounds for children and a funfair area. A monorail runs around the top and over the busy road, dropping you off at several stops. A lovely new building is nearly completed, it is a luxury hotel, complete with golden lions on the top of the structure, replicas of the San Marco lions on the cathedral in Venice. There is also a school which caters for the offspring of these returned Chinese. Some of them come to our school in Nanshan, as we have the reputation of the best school in the Nanshan District.

Amidst all this splendour are the Hong Kong Chinese, Canadian and American Chinese, Taiwanese and others, who have emigrated and returned to do business deals with the motherland. These wealthy individuals put their money together to create this overseas Chinese area. It is also well patronised by tour groups mainly from Hong Kong but includes visitors from around the world.

Across the road, within a mile of each other, are three famous theme parks, 'The Windows of the World', 'Splendid China' and 'The Ethnic Villages'.

For visitors with limited time, the Splendid China park gives a good idea of the famous sights and buildings throughout China. You can walk or travel on motorised vehicles around the large park, which has big models of the Terracotta Warriors, famous grottos with Buddha figures, a replica of the Great Wall, big enough to pose on for photographs, The Yellow Crane Tower of Wuhan and so on.

'The Windows of the World' is more for the Chinese

visitors. Here they can see the wonders of the western buildings such as the Eiffel Tower, the Taj Mahal, the Pyramids in Egypt, even the Niagara Falls. Facing onto the main road, you can clearly see the colourful houses of Holland. There are fountains and huge balloons, with banners describing in Chinese characters and English the forthcoming attractions. Dancers, singers and entertainers from around the world come to live and work here for a few weeks to perform in daily shows. Every weekend they have a grande finale with a firework display. I can watch this from my bedroom window in Nanshan. It is fun to watch and listen to these regular, free, colourful shows, huge bursts of red, green, gold and blue stars exploding into the night sky, often with a moon brighter than the fireworks over the mountains.

My favourite of these three theme parks, is The Ethnic Villages. Here live the ethnic people from all different parts of China. They live in authentically-built houses and wear the costumes of their region and ethnic origin. They carry on with their usual daily lives and you are invited to talk and visit them in their homes. At set times, to the noise of a thousand drums, or so it sounds, you can go and watch the many different dances from each ethnic group. The costumes are wonderful, the dances well performed and the park beautiful with lakes and weeping willow trees, plants and flowers. Small shops sell ethnic souvenirs, these can be bargained down and are quite reasonable. Outside the parks are many open stall shops, these are usually more expensive. Good buys are the ethnic, woven-cloth shoulder bags and purses. Wall hangings of flowers, mountains etc are available and roll easily to carry on planes. Fans, hats and toys for children are numerous and inexpensive. If you speak Chinese, you can always get a good bargain.

This area has a holiday atmosphere and is popular

with local Chinese families at the weekends.

When we first came to Shenzhen from UK and then Hong Kong, we wanted a base from which to explore before we met our new unit leaders. As we knew from past experience, once you join them everything is organised for you, whether you want it or not.

I looked in a guide book in England and chose a hotel at random, having no idea where our school was situated.

Luckily I chose the Shenzhen Bay, which advertised a swimming pool and landscaped gardens. This hotel is part of the overseas Chinese complex. It was ideal for a couple of nights for us to acclimatise to the fierce heat. The gardens are truly beautiful. Set around several swimming pools and waterfalls, little paths lead you across small bridges, over streams full of croaking frogs and lotus flowers. There are lovely, small palm trees, rubber plants, thickets of slender bamboo and banana trees full of fruit. It is the ideal place to relax, especially in, out-of-season months.

Inside are both Chinese and Western restaurants.

Many activities took place in the months leading up to the hand over of Hong Kong from Britain. One of these was a mass wedding of hundreds of couples all together at the Shenzhen Bay Hotel. We watched them as they came out of the ceremony and onto the courtyard outside, posing for many reporters, photographers and television cameras, the brides resplendent in their white dresses and veils, the grooms in full morning dress, it was a happy scene. They were given free access to the hotel, and all surrounding theme parks for the day. Special concerts were performed for them and it all cost them a fraction of the normal wedding fees.

We enjoyed our visits to Shenzhen Bay, although as our busy school life evolved, different times and experiences lay ahead.

# Chapter 15

## The End of the Rainbow

The end of the rainbow for me has been the fruitful blossoming of a creative, interactive classroom, which I was allowed to design and use exclusively with all the eleven classes I taught at the Nanshan Foreign Language School. Having patiently followed the Chinese system and slowly showed the Western ways of teaching via many demonstration classes and teacher training lectures, the Nanshan Education Bureau were happy to give the go-ahead for us to try some different approaches. As the school is called an experimental school, it is allowed to try out many new things to improve standards. Once approved, then the system or ideas are incorporated in schools throughout Shenzhen and Guangdong Province.

Many officials called to watch and interview the staff and children, including top education officials from Beijing and from many different countries. TV programmes helped to promote the school, until the waiting list became impossible. Before the start of each new term, hundreds of parents and small toddlers queued outside the school gates, waiting for an interview and papers to fill in, to give a chance for their child to come to Nanshan Foreign Language School. The selection procedure involved the chosen few to have an entrance examination. As the children were very young these were not difficult, but the parents were also under scrutiny. What were their jobs? Did they fit the school's image? etc. A lot of Gwanxi (a favour in return for another) went on in the early days, a question of who knew who and what benefits could they bring to the school.

This system happens all over China as in the West. If your face fits (and your pocket) you're in with a good chance.

The school is mostly funded by the Chinese Government and it depends upon its yearly performance as to how much money it will be allocated. Competitions abound throughout the school year. All subjects, their teachers and school upkeep have regular inspections and a constant stream of visitors. The pupils rise to each occasion, especially during demonstration classes. Concerts are lavish, sometimes held in big theatres belonging to the big companies on the Science and Industry Park. They are also sponsors for many school projects and award medals, prize money, gifts and certificates. Parties are often given for the school staff by these companies, in recognition of their work in the community. Prizes are given for raffles. I have won or been presented with whole dinner services, coffee sets, blankets, toiletries, certificates etc. Every teacher gets something even if it is a bar of soap.

The incentives are there and good teachers are well rewarded, often with an unexpected money bonus.

The parents are a mixture of Chinese peasants, who became rich by selling their fishing ground to builders for white-collar workers and University professors. Nanshan district was a small fishing village fifteen to twenty years ago. It is unrecognisable today via its spectacular new-age architecture and Spanish and Italian style estates, with pink and white, green and blue stucco villas.

Each estate has electronic gates, with guards at each entrance and exit. Passes must be shown as you walk through to visit a friend or a sleek car passes through. There is money in this part of China and big global deals are made here. The stock market is booming and has two types of shares A and B, one for Chinese and one for foreigners. Recently, B shares can by bought by anyone.

Several of our teachers held 'A' shares from which they mostly made a good profit. They were constantly on their mobile phones after classes, in order to check the daily share indexes.

We preferred to watch and listen on the local television, without active participation, a wise move as the shares plunged dramatically while we were in Shenzhen!

The Chinese love a gamble, be it on the stock market or a game of cards, it certainly gave their live a sparkle.

# Chapter 16

## The Pot of Gold

For many people, working in Shenzhen is the pot of gold at the end of the rainbow. In China it represents five times the amount of money to be earned monthly. It has rules about who works in the area as so many want to come here. Teachers must pass special exams in order to be a Shenzhen citizen. Without this exam, teachers are poorly paid and can be sacked at a moment's notice. This does not inspire confidence in the workers, who jostle and vie for favour with the Heads and leaders. Insecurity makes hard workers but can also breed hostility. Many young men and women flock to the city looking for work and turn to petty crime. If caught, they will be severely punished and sent back to the countryside.

China has its rich pockets but this wealth must spread inwards to give poor areas better living conditions. The Government does what it can to alleviate the poorer areas and set up new industries where needed. The pay is still pitiful for farmers.

My pot of gold is not in money. (I could earn far more in the UK), but in the challenge of bringing and implementing new educational ideas which are working and in the joint exchange of ideas, culture and customs. It is not an easy life, but conditions in Shenzhen are what you make of it. Shenzhen is not the China of many people's imagination but it is the well-spring from which better educational opportunities will spread throughout the whole of China. The children of today are the future citizens of tomorrow. They hold the power to create stability and good communication with the rest of the world. They are the pot of gold at the end of the rainbow.